CAMPFIRE COOKBOOK

Delicious Recipes & Ideas for Making Meals

(All Recipes You Need for an Amazing Camping Trip)

John Jamar

Published by Alex Howard

© **John Jamar**

All Rights Reserved

Campfire Cookbook: Delicious Recipes & Ideas for Making Meals (All Recipes You Need for an Amazing Camping Trip)

ISBN 978-1-990169-42-7

All rights reserved. No part of this guide may be reproduced in any form without permission in writing from the publisher except in the case of brief quotations embodied in critical articles or reviews.

Legal & Disclaimer

The information contained in this book is not designed to replace or take the place of any form of medicine or professional medical advice. The information in this book has been provided for educational and entertainment purposes only.

The information contained in this book has been compiled from sources deemed reliable, and it is accurate to the best of the Author's knowledge; however, the Author cannot guarantee its accuracy and validity and cannot be held liable for any errors or omissions. Changes are periodically made to this book. You must consult your doctor or get professional medical advice before using any of the suggested remedies, techniques, or information in this book.

Table of contents

PART 1 1

INTRODUCTION 2

BREAKFAST RECIPES 3

BREAKFAST BURRITOS 3
FRENCH TOAST 4
HOT HAM & SWISS CROISSANTS 5
HAM AND PINEAPPLE SANDWICHES 6

LUNCH RECIPES 7

CHICKEN AND POTATO FOIL PACKET 7
WHITE BEAN CHICKEN PACKETS 8
BBQ PACK 9
CHICKEN-AND-RICE 11
BBQ CHICKEN FOIL PACKS 12
TACO PATTIES & POTATOES FOIL PACKET 13

DINNER RECIPES 14

GRILLED CHICKEN AND VEGETABLES IN FOIL 14
SOUTHWESTERN CHICKEN FOIL PACKET 15
LIME WHITE FISH PACKETS 16
LEMON GRILLED SHRIMP 18
GRILLED FISH FOIL PACKETS 19
CAMPING MAC N' CHEESE 21

SNACKS 22

FOIL-PACK CHEESY FRIES 22
STREET CORN OVER THE CAMPFIRE 23
PESTO CATFISH PACKETS 24
FOIL PACKET HOT DOG 25
HERB STEAK FOIL PACKET 26
DESSERT RECIPES 27
ROASTED CARAMEL PEACHES WITH PECANS 28

Tin Foil Monkey Bread	29
Campfire Pies	30
The "Girl Scouts Breakfast"	32
Chilli Rice	33
Campfire Steak	34
BBQ Sandwiches	35
Fire BBQ Pita's	36
Beef In The Wild	37
Beef Can Soup	38
No Taco Tacos	39
One Pot Dinner	40
Easy Mac N Cheese	41
Mexican Casserole	42
Camping Stew	43
Smores In A Cone	44
Burritos	45
Dutch Oven Potato's	46
Pizza Nachos	47
Campfire Éclairs	48

KABOBS IN A BAG 49

Chicken Or Beef	49
Part 2	51

CAMPFIRE COOKING 52

A "Girl Scouts" Breakfast	52
All In One Potato Frittata	53
Apple Pie On A Stick	54
Baby Red Potatoes	55
Backwoods Chili Rice Skillet	56
Bacon & Cheddar Grilled Cheese Sandwich	57
Bag Kabobs	58
Baked Apples	59
Baked Onions	60
Baked Pancakes	61
Baked Potato In A Can	62

Balsamic Steak	63
Balsamic Vinegar Chicken	64
Banana Boat	65
Banana Boats	66
Banana Chocolate Chip Split	67
Bar-B-Que Bean Bake	68
BBQ Pitas	69
BBQ Potato Chips	70
BBQ Ribs	71
Beef In The Wild	73
Berry Pie	74
Big Jim's Camping Beans	75
Biscuits On A Stick	76
Blair's Campfire Stew	77
Blondies	78
Bratwurts & Swiss	79
Breakfast Bag	80
BREAKFAST BURRITO	**81**
Breakfast Burritos With Sausage	82
Brown Bears	83
Brunswick Stew	84
Buger & Veggie Pouches	85
Cajun Shrimp Gumbo	86
Camp Beef Brisket	87
Camp Bread	88
Camp Eclairs	89
Camp Fruit Cobbler	90
Camp Stew	91
Camp Stove Goulash	92
Camp Taters	93
Camper's Luau Chicken	94
Camper's Pizza Skillet Delight	95
Camper's Skillet	96
Campers Stew	97
Campfire Chicken & Vegetables	98

Campfire Chicken & Veggies	99
Campfire Chicken Pot Pie	100
Campfire Chili With Hamburger	101
Campfire Chili	102
Campfire Corn	103
Campfire Delights	104
Campfire Dessert Wraps	105
Campfire Dinner	106
Campfire Eggs	107
Campfire French Fries	108
Campfire Fudge	109
Campfire Onion	110
Campfire Pineapple Upsidedown Cakes	111
Campfire Potatoes And Onions	112
Campfire Potatoes	113
Campfire Roasted Turkey	114
Campfire Stew With Hamburger	115
Campfire Stew	116
Campfire Stir Fry	117
Campfire Sweet Potatoes	118
Campfire Tacos	119
Campground Chicken Salad	120
Camping Margarita's	121
Camping Potatoes	122
Camping Rice Pudding	123
Camping Spaghetti	124
Camping Stew	125
Camp-Out Tomatoes	126
Cheddar Spam & Potatoes	127
Cheese On The Cob	128
Cheesy Veggie Chowder	129
Cherry Dessert	130
Chicken Asparagus	131
Chicken Cacciatore	132
Chicken In A Bag	133
Chicken Pie	134

Chicken Salsa Stir-Fry	135
Chip-A-S'mores	136
Chocolate-Peanut Butter Wraps	137
Chuck Wagon	138
Chunky Chill Chaser	139
Citrus Trout	140
Clam Chowder	141
Coconut Lime Layer Cake	142
Coffee Can Chicken	143
Corn On The Cob With Bacon	144
Corn On The Cob	145
Corn Roasted In Foil On Coals	146
Corn Roasted On Girl Over Coals	147
Cornish Game Hen	148
Cowboy Stew	149
Cowboy Turn Spit Game Hens	149
Cream Cheese Chicken	150
Crockpot Vegetable Beef Soup	150
Crunchy Oriental Coleslaw Salad	151
Darrell's Mexican Casserole	151
Day Camp Stew	152
Delicious Poached Salmon	152
Deluxe Steamed Green Beans	153
Deviled Eggs	154
Dilled Peas & Potatoes	154
Doctored Up Pork & Beans	155
Dog Gone Good Doggies	155
Donuts Surprise!	156
Dutch Oven Chicken	156
Dutch Oven Cobbler	156
Dutch Oven Stuffed Peppers	157
Easy Barbecue Sauce	158
Easy Campfire Corn	158
Easy Campfire Mushrooms	159
Easy Campfire Peach Cobbler	159
Easy Campfire Pizza	159

Easy Campfire Stew	160
Easy Home Pries	160
Easy Pigs'n A Blanket	161
Easy Rice Recipe	161
Esay Taco Salad	162
Easy Taco Soup	162
Easy Tostadas	163
Eggs In A Bag	163
Fire Pit Potatoes	164
Fireside Fajita's	164
Fish In Foil	165
Fish Packets For Four	165
Foil Bag Surprise	166
Foil Dinner For One	166
Foolproof Roast Chicken	167
Fresh Fruit Cake	168
Frogmore Stew	169
Fruit Compote In Foil	170
Fruit Kabobs	171
Garbage	171
Girl Scouts Banana Dessert	172
Golden Parmesan Potatoes	172
Gorp	173
Grandma's Easy Camping Taco	173
Great Omelet	173
Grilled Apple Rings	174
Grilled Apples In Apple Brandy	175
Grilled BBQ Meatloaf	175
Grilled Breakfast Sandwich	175
Grilled Marinated Shark Steaks	176
Grilled Peanut Butter Sandwiches	176
Grilled Peppers	177
Grilled Pineapple	177
Grilled Pizza	178
Grilled Potatoes	178
Grilled Shrimp	178

GRILLED SQUASH & ZUCCHINI	179
GRILLED SQUASH	179
GRILLED VEGIES	180
GRINGO GORDY'S GRILLED VEGGIES	180
HAM & SWEET POTATO FOIL PACKETS	181
HAMBURGER HOBO PIE	181
HAMBURGER STEW	182
HAMBURGER-RICE CASSEROLE	183
HASH BROWN CASSEROLE	183
HEATHER'S CAMPFIRE CHICKEN PARMESAN	184
HILDEBRANDT FAMILY CAMPFIRE POTATOES	184
HILLBILLY STEW	185
HOBO BURGERS	185
HOBO CHICKEN	186
HOBO DINNER	186
HOBO POTATOES	187
HOBO SQUARES	188

Part 1

Introduction

Just because you are out in the woods on the campground does not mean that you should just eat canned foods. You will be happy to know that you can have a hot tasty meal even in the woods. Did you know that you could actually prepare delicious meals in a foil? Wouldn't it be great to be able to prepare meals without having to deal with dirty utensils? If you want to learn more about foil packet cooking, you are in the right place.

This book will provide you with mouth-watering breakfast, lunch, dinner, snacks and dessert recipes that you can prepare in a foil. These recipes are simple and take a relatively short time to prepare. Thanks to this book, camping cooking has been taken to a completely new level.

Thanks again for downloading this book, I hope you enjoy it!

Breakfast Recipes

Breakfast Burritos

Serves: 8

Ingredients
8 (12-inch) flour tortillas
¼ cup chopped cilantro
2 cups (8 ounce) cheddar cheese, shredded
1 (4.5 ounce) can green chilies
1 tablespoon taco seasoning
12 eggs
8 ounce cooked ham, diced
1 cup frozen hash browns
½ tablespoon olive oil

Directions
1. In a large skillet, heat some oil and then add in the hash browns. Cook them for about a minute, while stirring frequently.
2. Add in the ham and cook for around 8 to 10 minutes, or until the ham and the hash browns have browned.
3. As the mixture cooks, lightly whisk the eggs in a large bowl. Whisk in taco seasoning and wait for the mixture to brown, and then pour in the eggs in the ham-hash brown mixture.
4. Cook the egg mixture until the eggs are cooked through, while stirring as required. Then stir in cheese, green chiles and cilantro.
5. Warm the tortillas then put about one-eighth of the egg mixture in the center of each warm tortilla.
6. Roll up into a burrito and wrap tightly in a foil. Store the wrap in a ziptop bag in a cooler.
7. Once ready to cook, put the burritos in hot coals near the fire. Allow the burritos to cook in the coal for about 10 to 15 minutes, turning once.
8. Once heated through, remove from fire and serve.

French Toast

Serves: 6

Ingredients

1 500g container of fresh strawberries
¼ cup sliced almonds
1 carton of Burn-brae Farms French Toast Egg Creations
1 loaf of bread of choice
Syrup of choice
Confectioners' sugar

Directions

1. Wash the berries, slice half of the container and dice the other half.
2. Using a parchment paper, wrap a loaf of bread and then foil loosely to the point that bread slices can fall slightly open.
3. Sprinkle all the diced berries over the bread slices, mostly between the slices. Reserve the remaining sliced berries for use later.
4. Sprinkle sliced almonds on the bread particularly between the slices. Wrap the parchment paper and foil tighter around the bread.
5. Pour the toast eggs over the bread and wrap tightly using a foil to ensure the mixture doesn't leak.
6. Put the package on a grill or campfire and cook for 35 to 40 minutes on low to medium heat, while turning around now and then. Cook for longer in case you find the bread soggy.
7. Once cooked through, remove from heat and let it sit for 10 minutes and then serve with sliced strawberries, syrup or sugar.

Hot Ham & Swiss Croissants

Serves 4

Ingredients

8 slices Swiss cheese
4 croissants split
1 tablespoon brown sugar
1 tablespoon honey
2 tablespoons Dijon mustard

Directions

1. Combine brown sugar, honey and the mustard. Spread this mixture on each side of the four split crescent-shaped rolls (croissants).
2. Put a slice of cheese on each half of the croissants and top the bottom of each bread roll with sufficient amount of ham.
3. Put the two halves together and wrap in a foil to form a packet.
4. To cook, place in a preheated grill until heated through and then serve. Enjoy!

Ham And Pineapple Sandwiches

Serves 6

Ingredients

1 tablespoon honey
2 tablespoon Dijon mustard
6 slices cheddar cheese
6 pineapple rings, cut in half if desired
9 ounce deli sliced ham
6 Artisan French Rolls

Directions

1. Cut the French rolls in half and set aside. Mix honey and Dijon mustard then spread the mixture on the bottom of each roll.
2. Layer the sandwich by folding a few ham pieces and put them on top of the honey mixture.
3. Top the ham with a pineapple ring, preferably cut in half if you like it. Top the pineapple ring with cheddar cheese slices, and then top with half of the French roll.
4. Wrap each of the sandwiches serving with aluminum foil. Once done, put the sandwiches over a grill rack or hot coal for about 20 minutes.
5. After cooking time elapse, unwrap the foil packet and serve the sandwiches.

Lunch Recipes

Chicken And Potato Foil Packet

Serves 5

Ingredients
Shredded cheddar cheese
BBQ sauce
1 small bag of small golden potatoes
2 pounds of boneless skinless chicken tenderloins
Salt and Pepper to taste
Olive oil

Directions
1. Cut the potatoes into smaller pieces and pack them evenly in 5 foil packets along with pepper, salt and olive oil.
2. Fold the packets up, and leave some room at the top for steaming. Close the side of the packet tightly and cook for around 15 minutes.
3. Once cooked through, remove the foil from the grill and add in 2 to 3 chicken pieces to the opened packets and sufficient amount of BBQ sauce.
4. Seal the packets again and cook for another 15 to 25 minutes. Remove from the grill and periodically check if the chicken is ready.
5. As soon as the packets are cooked through, add some cheddar cheese and then serve.

White Bean Chicken Packets

Serves 4

Ingredients

1/2 cup shredded Mexican blend cheese
1 tablespoon Mexican spice blend
4 chicken breasts, boneless and skinless
1 can of corn bits
1 (10 ounce) can of drained diced tomatoes
1 (15 ounce) can of navy beans drained and rinsed
Chopped green onion to top
4 tin foil squares about 18" x 12"

Directions

1. In a large bowl, mix all ingredients apart from the green onion and cheese.
2. Put a quarter of the mixture in each foil square, and then fold up to prevent the mixture from leaking.
3. Put the foil packet on the grill or grate and cook for 20 to 25 minutes. Turn the packet a couple of times for even cooking.
4. As soon as the chicken is cooked through, remove from the campfire and cool for a moment.
5. Remove the foil packets onto a plate and top with the onion and cheese.

Bbq Pack

Serves 2 -4

Ingredients

4- 12 pieces x8" of foil or just large squares
1/2 teaspoon ground coriander
1 teaspoon chili powder ancho
1 teaspoon smoked paprika
1 teaspoon ground cumin
1 1/2 teaspoons onion powder
1/2 teaspoon black pepper
1 teaspoon lemon juice
2 teaspoons liquid smoke
3/4 teaspoon sea salt
2 teaspoons olive oil
1 cob of corn sliced into 1" wide medallions
1 cup button or baby bella mushrooms, chopped
1 cup zucchini chopped
1 cup russet potato, cut into 1/2" pieces
1 cup carrots, cut into 1/2" pieces
1 cup red or white onion chopped
1 cup red/orange bell peppers, chopped

Optional

Chickpeas
Smoked tofu seitan

Directions

1. Heat the grill over medium heat and then put the ingredients in a large bowl.
2. Toss the mixture together to coat. Now distribute the mixture among 4 foil pieces, approximately a cup in each. Put in the center of the foil.
3. At Fold two sides of the foil around the center and continue folding down until you get to the veggies. Press the contents flat.
4. Get one of the other sides and roll into the center, and repeat on all sides until you form a packet. Press the folds or rolls firmly to ensure they don't come out.

5. Place them on the grill, cover and cook each side of the packet for about 8 minutes. To check if ready, peel back a fold and then check either the potato or corn.

6. To get a drier mixture, try opening the top of the packets during cooking approximately 4 minutes before cook time is over.

7. Serve it hot while topped with pepper and salt, BBQ sauce or hot sauce if you like.

Chicken-And-Rice

Serves 4

Ingredients

2 scallions, thinly sliced
2 cups low-sodium chicken broth
Kosher salt
1/4 teaspoon turmeric
1 teaspoon chili powder
1 tablespoon tomato paste
2 tablespoons pickled jalapeno slices, finely chopped
1 cup salsa
1 cup converted rice
1 (15-ounce) can black beans, drained and rinsed
4 chicken thighs, cut into 1/2-inch chunks
4 8-inch disposable foil pie pans
Heavy duty foil

Directions

1. First, heat the grill to medium high heat.
2. Place the chicken thighs, chili powder, tomato paste, pickled jalapenos, salsa, rice, beans, salt and turmeric powder in a big bowl. Toss to combine the ingredients.
3. Distribute the rice and chicken thigh mixture among the four pie pans, and spread the mixture in a layer.
4. Pour about half a cup of chicken broth into each pan and now cover each of the pie pans with foil.
5. Place the pan on the grill, seal the lid and cook until the meat is cooked through, or about 20 minutes. Then remove from heat and let it rest for a moment.
6. Once cooled, remove the foil from each pie pan and check if all the liquids have been absorbed and rice tender.
7. Sprinkle with scallions and enjoy.

Bbq Chicken Foil Packs

Serves 4

Ingredients

1 small red onion, diced
1 red bell pepper, diced
2 cups drained pineapple tidbits
2 cups barbecue sauce
4 chicken breasts, cut in 1-inch pieces

Directions

1. Preheat your grill. Meanwhile cut 4 large sheets of aluminum and arrange them singly on a flat ground.
2. Toss together barbecue sauce and the chicken breast cut into one-inch pieces in a medium bowl until the meat is fully coated.
3. Divide the meat pieces among the sheets of aluminum foil. Divide 2 cups of pineapple tidbits, 1 small onion and a bell pepper evenly on the foil.
4. Bring up sides of the aluminum foil over the meat so that the edges meet. Seal edges to make a tight fold, but allow some space on the sides for steam expansion. Fold the sides to seal it properly.
5. Put the foil packs on the grill and cook for around 10 minutes. Turn the foils over and cook until the chicken juice is clear when its thickest part is cut, or for another 10 or 15 minutes.

Taco Patties & Potatoes Foil Packet

Serves 4 packets

Ingredients

1 cup cheesy salsa dip
3 cups diced hash brown potatoes
1/4 cup milk
2 tablespoons taco seasoning
1/2 cup plain breadcrumbs
1 pound lean ground beef or ground turkey
Salt & Pepper

Directions

1. Mix the milk, seasonings, breadcrumbs and the meat in a medium bowl until well incorporated.
2. Form about 4 patties from the dough, and make 4 double layer square foil and grease with cooking spray.
3. Put each patty on a single foil and then distribute the potatoes evenly on each double layer of foil.
4. Spread the taco patties on each foil packet and season with some pepper and salt.
5. Now spread the cheesy salsa over each foil contents: i.e. the patties and potatoes.
6. Wrap and completely seal the foil, but leave some room in the foil packet for air to flow through during cooking.
7. Cook on the grill or hot coal for about 15 to 20 minutes. Flip the mixture halfway through as it cooks.
8. Once done, open the foil packet carefully and then serve the cheesy potatoes.

Dinner Recipes

Grilled Chicken And Vegetables In Foil

Serves 4

Ingredients

8 asparagus spears
1 red, green or yellow bell pepper, cut into thin strips
1 zucchini, sliced into thin rounds
1/2 cup barbecue sauce
4 4-ounces boneless, skinless chicken breasts
8 large aluminum foil sheets
Extra virgin olive oil
Fresh ground pepper
Salt

Directions

1. Heat the grill to medium heat. For every foil pack, make 2 sheets of foil. Put one sheet on top of another.
2. Put the chicken meat on the foil sheets, and season with pepper and salt. Brush each breast using your favorite sauce.
3. Distribute equally and arrange the veggies around each breast, and then season with more pepper and salt.
4. Drizzle the veggies and chicken breast with olive oil. Fold the sides of the foil over the meat to cover the contents fully, and seal the packets.
5. Move the foil packets to the grill and cook until the contents are cooked through, or for about 20-25 minutes. The chicken breast should be done at 165 degrees F.
6. Let the cooked meat rest for a few minutes and then serve.

Southwestern Chicken Foil Packet

Serves 4

Ingredients

4 lime wedges
1 cup cheese blend, shredded
4 teaspoons taco seasoning
4 boneless, skinless chicken breasts
4 sprigs cilantro
4 heavy-duty aluminum foil, 18" x 12" long sheets
1 14.5 ounce can black beans, drained and rinsed
1 cup salsa, drained of excess moisture
1 cup corn kernels
Salt and pepper

Directions

1. Heat your grill to medium heat. Stir together beans, salsa and corn in a large bowl until well blended.
2. Put 4 pieces of foil on the counter and coat with cooking spray. Distribute the veggie mixture over the 4 packets and add 1 sprig of cilantro in each.
3. Season all sides of the chicken meat with pepper and salt along with a teaspoon of taco per each piece of meat. Put the seasoned chicken breasts on the vegetables.
4. Now fold the sides off the foil and bring the edges together, and then roll the foil until you get an allowance of 1 to 2 inches from the top of the meat.
5. Fold the short ends to seal the packets, but leaving some little space for steam to expand.
6. Put the packets on the grill and cook until the center of the meat is no longer pink, or for around 20 minutes.
7. Once cooked through, remove from the grill and let steam to escape. Season each packet with same amount of cheese, and seal the foil again.
8. Let the packets rest for around two minutes, or for longer until the cheese melts.
9. Finally serve the chicken with lime wedges.

Lime White Fish Packets

Serves 2

Ingredients

1 tablespoon fresh cilantro, chopped
6 ounces cod
1 tablespoon lime zest
½ cup light coconut milk
3 tablespoons olive oil
1 organic zucchini, halved and thinly sliced
2 cloves garlic, minced
1 shallot, halved and thinly sliced
1 cup organic sweet corn kernels, fresh (2 ears) or frozen
Black pepper, freshly ground
Salt

Directions

1. Preheat the grill to about 400 to 425 degrees F. Meanwhile pick two large squares of foil, measuring 10 inches in length.
2. Fold each of the foil in half to make a fold line, then open to resemble a book.
3. Layer equal amounts of corn, zucchini, garlic and shallot in the center of right half of each aluminum, near where you placed the fold line.
4. Fold up the sides of the right half of aluminum foil to create a bowl that holds the veggies.
5. To each of the packet, add in half tablespoon of lime zest, ¼ cup of milk and 1 ½ tablespoons of oil.
6. Season the mixture with salt and pepper and then mix together the ingredients with your hands.
7. Now cut the fish into two portions and put them onto the vegetables. Season the meat with pepper and salt.
8. Fold over the left half of aluminum foil and cover the mixture. Roll the top half of the foil along with the edges of the right half. Seal all edges to make an air-tight foil packet.

9. Put the packets with the right side facing up on a sheet then move it onto the preheated grill. Cook the fish for 8 to 10 minutes and then flip each packet using a spatula. Cook the other side for about 10 minutes or so.

10. Once cooked through, remove the foil packets from the grill using a spatula, and flip so that the right side with the fish is up. Set to a plate.

11. Cut a slit through the top center of each packet open using a knife or kitchen shears. Open the packet carefully taking care not to br burnt by the hot steam.

12. Check if the fish is opaque and well cooked in the center and if not return to the grill for another 8 or 10 minutes. If cooked through, top with chopped cilantro and veggies.

13. Serve the pockets in the foil to retain the flavors from the lime broth.

Lemon Grilled Shrimp

Serves
Ingredients
1 loaf French bread, for dipping
1 lemon
3 cloves fresh garlic, chopped
¼ cup fresh chives, chopped
½ stick butter, softened
1 pound shrimp, with shells, but deveined
Directions
1. Start by preparing the herb butter. Just mix together the chives, garlic and softened butter. Add in zest from half a lemon and stir to blend.
2. Now cut two big pieces of foil and lay them on top of each other to ensure none of the butter sauce run out.
3. Pick the shrimp and arrange half of the raw shrimp at the center of the middle of pieces of aluminum foil.
4. Pick half of the butter mixture and put it on top of the fish. At this point roll the center of the foil and roll on all sides until you create a secure foil pouch.
5. Repeat all the steps for the other half of the shellfish to have two pouches in case you are using one pound of shrimp.
6. Put the shrimp onto a preheated grill and cook for about 8 minutes; do not cook for any longer so as not to overcook.
7. Serve the shrimp with crusty French bread, fresh lemon slices and garnish with chives.

Grilled Fish Foil Packets

Serves 2

Ingredients

3 tablespoons basil, chopped
½ teaspoon onion powder
1 tablespoon dry white wine
2½ tablespoons olive oil
2 cloves garlic, minced
8 ounces cherry tomatoes, sliced
8 ounces wild cod
Black pepper, freshly ground
Salt

Directions

1. Begin by heating the grill to about 400 degrees F or medium-high heat. Tear off two squares of foil that measure 10 inches long.
2. Fold each aluminum foil in half to create a fold line, then open to resemble a book.
3. Now cut the cod into two portions and put one piece in the center of each foil, near the fold.
4. Layer equal amounts of garlic and tomato over each cod, and season with sufficient amount of pepper and salt.
5. Fold up the sides of the left half of the aluminum foil to make a kind of a "bowl". Then whisk together onion powder, wine and olive oil until well blended.
6. At this point drizzle olive oil mixture over the tomatoes and cod and then fold over the right half of aluminum foil to cover the food.
7. Taking enough care, roll the top half of the aluminum foil together with the edges of the left foil and seal all edges. Create an airtight packet.
8. Put the packet with the tomatoes on top, i.e. right side up on the grill. Cook the fish packets for around 10 minutes.
9. Once ready, remove the packets from the grill using a spatula, and set onto a plate.

10. Slit through the top of each foil packet using a knife or kitchen shears and carefully open the packets.
11. In case the cod is not cooked through, return to the grill and cook for about 5 to 7 minutes.
12. Top the cod with chopped basil and serve the fish right in the foil. Enjoy!

Camping Mac N' Cheese

Serves 4

Ingredients

1/4-1/2 cup half and half or whole milk
1/4 cup mozzarella cheese
1/2 cup grated Parmesan cheese
1/2 cup grated sharp cheddar cheese
8 ounce prepared Alfredo sauce
1 1/2 cups elbow macaroni
Pepper
Salt

Directions

1. Begin by cooking the pasta following the package directions, then drain and rinse in cold water.
2. Into the cooked pasta, stir in Alfred sauce along with sufficient milk and the three cheeses. Season the mixture with pepper and salt.
3. Distribute the mixture among 4 pie tins that are coated with non-stick cooking spray. Coat one side of foil with spray and cover each of the pie tins sprayed side facing the mac and cheese.
4. Seal the pie tins fully and store them in a plastic food storage bag in a freezer or cooler until ready to cook.
5. Make a fire and let it burn down to the coals. Put a cooking rack on top about 2 to 3 inches above.
6. Put each of the pie tin over the coal and cook until hot or for 8 to 10 minutes. Once cooked through, remove from the coal and serve.

Snacks

Foil-Pack Cheesy Fries

Serves 4

Ingredients
2 tablespoons real bacon bits, cooked
2 tablespoons sliced green onions
4 slices American cheese
1 tablespoon butter, melted
1 bag (14 ounce) frozen French fries

Directions
1. Heat a charcoal grill or gas over medium heat, and then toss the melted butter with frozen French fries.
2. Tear off two foils and make foil boats. Put half of the fries in a single layer in the center of a foil then loosely fold around the edges to make a boat. Leave a large hole at the top for steam to escape through.
3. Repeat the procedure with the other foil and remaining fries. Now put the foil packet on the grill, cover and cook for about 20 to 30 minutes but over indirect heat.
4. Stir once and cook until the fries are crispy. Top with 2 slices of cheese. If need be, cook for another 2 minutes or until baked through.
5. To serve, sprinkle with bacon bits and sliced green onions and enjoy.

Street Corn Over The Campfire

Serves 6

Ingredients

2 fresh limes juiced
1 cup parmesan cheese, freshly grated
1/2 cup fresh cilantro, finely chopped
2 cups sour cream
3/4 cup mayo
6 ears of corn
Chili powder to taste

Directions

1. First, husk the corn or instead leave the ends on.
2. Grill the ears of corn over the campfire while turning occasionally to avoid burning the corn, until lightly charred.
3. Meanwhile, combine cilantro, sour cream and mayo in a bowl.
4. Now remove the corn from the campfire and season with the mayo seasoning.
5. Allow the corn to cool then season with lime juice, and then sprinkle cheese and some chili powder. Serve and enjoy.

Pesto Catfish Packets

Serves 8

Ingredients

Lime slices
1 pint cherry tomatoes cut into halves
Black pepper, freshly ground
1 1/2 teaspoons salt
1/2 cup jarred pesto
8 (6-ounce) catfish fillets
1/4 cup extra-virgin olive oil

Directions

1. Preheat the grill over medium high heat, and then cut 8 pieces of foil, measuring approximately 8 by 11 inches.
2. Drizzle some oil over each piece of foil and put the catfish fillets on top of oil. Spread about 1 tablespoon of pesto over each fish fillet.
3. Season with salt and pepper then top with lime slices and tomatoes.
4. Seal the packets and put onto the preheated grill's rack. Cook until the fish are opaque, or for about 10 minutes.

Foil Packet Hot Dog

Serves 3

Ingredients

Salt and Pepper to taste
Olive oil
3 fingerling potatoes, sliced thin
1/2 small onion, sliced thinly
1/2 red pepper sliced
1 pack Hebrew National Hot Dogs
Aluminum foil

Directions

1. Cut off large square aluminum foils and then put 1 to 3 hotdogs in each foil square.
2. Put sliced veggies on top of the hot dogs and drizzle oil over the hotdogs. Season the food with pepper and salt.
3. Now fold the aluminum foils into small envelopes and grill them on preheated grill until the veggies are cooked through, in about 15 to 20 minutes.

Herb Steak Foil Packet

Serves 1 packet
Ingredients
1 sprig fresh rosemary
1/2 lemon
1 thin cut steak such as rib-eye
Butter & Olive Oil
Pepper
Dried Thyme
Salt
Asparagus, optional
Heavy Duty Foil – 2 sheets
Directions
1. First, heat the coals on your campfire or preheat your grill to medium high heat.
2. Grease 12 by 12 inch heavy duty foil with a dot of butter mixed with olive oil.
3. Season the steak with pepper and salt and then put it in the center of the heavy duty foil. Season the meat with thyme, slice of lemon and rosemary leaves.
4. Place the lemon and fresh veggies next to the steak, dot with some butter and then cover the mixture with the second piece of foil.
5. Completely seal the foil and then put the foil packet on the grill. Cook until the steak is cooked through, or for about 8 to 10 minutes; while flipping halfway during cook time.
6. Once done, allow the steak to sit for 2 to 3 minutes before opening the foil.

Dessert Recipes

Apple Pie Packets
Serves 1
Ingredients
1 tablespoon chopped pecans
1 tablespoon raisins or dried cranberries
1/4 teaspoon ground cinnamon
1 1/2 tablespoon brown sugar
1 tablespoon butter
1 apple, cored and sliced
Directions
1. Heat the grill to medium heat and then cut about 12 by 18 inch of a foil.
2. Put dried cranberries, cinnamon, brown sugar and apple slices on the non-stick foil.
3. Now wrap to secure using double-fold seals, but do not allow any room for contents to expand.
4. Put the package on the preheated grill, cover and cook over medium heat for around 15 minutes.
5. Once cooked through, remove from the grill carefully using a grill-safe spatula to scoop up the packet. Set it onto a plate before serving.
6. If you want, you can serve it hot; carefully open the packets, as there will be hot steam as you open. Serve it in the packets and enjoy.
7. In case you notice juices at the bottom of the packet, stir in the apple around the juices and enjoy.

Roasted Caramel Peaches With Pecans

Serves 2

Ingredients

2 peaches, ripe but firm
1/4 cup pecan halves
2 tablespoons caramel sauce
1 teaspoon butter

Directions

1. Burn the campfire down to the coals or instead preheat the grill over medium high heat.
2. Grease a large aluminum foil with butter and spoon 1 tablespoon of brown sugar or caramel.
3. Scatter the pecans over the brown sugar or caramel and set aside. Meanwhile, wash the peaches and slice them in half, and then remove the pit.
4. Layer 4 peach halves, the cut side facing down on the pecans. Drizzle the pecans with the remainder of caramel sauce.
5. Wrap the peaches up tightly and put in a low grill or hot campfire. Cook until cooked through or for 20 to 25 minutes.
6. Once done, remove from the campfire or grill and let the steam to escape and for the dessert to cool. Invert the cooled dessert onto a plate and allow any excess liquids to drain.
7. Serve the caramel peaches and enjoy!

Tin Foil Monkey Bread

Makes 2 tin foil packets

Ingredients

3/4 cup brown sugar
4 tablespoon cold butter
1 can biscuits
1 teaspoon cinnamon
1/4 cup sugar

Directions

1. Spray a non-stick cooking spray on two tin foils and set them aside.
2. Stir together cinnamon and sugar. Cut each of the biscuits into four and roll the pieces into the sugar-cinnamon mixture.
3. Now divide the biscuit pieces among two foil packets. Cut the butter into smaller cube-shaped pieces.
4. Sprinkle the butter cubes between the two foil packets and top with brown sugar. Then seal the foil packets by sealing up the edges.
5. Cook the bread over hot coals until the biscuits are cooked through, in about 20 minutes. Ensure you turn the contents occasionally to facilitate even cooking.

Campfire Pies

Serves 2-4

Ingredients

2 tablespoons cinnamon sugar mixture
4 bread slices
Handful blueberries, peach slices or apple slices
Nonstick cooking spray
Aluminum foils

Directions

1. Preheat the campfire to very hot with glowing charcoal. Meanwhile, grease aluminum foil with cooking spray.
2. Put a piece of loaf in each side of the foil and press it down lightly to create an indentation on the loaf of bread.
3. Put a few tablespoons of seasonal fruits such as blueberries on the bread and sprinkle with a tablespoon of sugar cinnamon mixture. Lay the other pieces of the loaf on top of one another.
4. Now wrap the sides of the foil to form a foil packet and slightly press it down so as to lock the sides together.
5. Scrap away any bread bits that hang out of the foil as they can burn in the hot coals. Put the foil package in the hottest part of campfire and let it cook for 2 to 3 minutes.
4. Once the sides are toasted and become golden brown, carefully remove the hot foil package from campfire. Let cool for a few minutes and then serve.

Un-Baked Cookies

1/2 cup of softened butter
2/3 cups of white sugar
3 tbsp. unsweetened cocoa powder
1 tbsp. strong brewed coffee
1/2 tsp. of vanilla extract
1 3/4 cups of rolled oats
1/3 cup confectioners' sugar

Instructions

Mix butter, sugar, cocoa, coffee and vanilla together in a bowl.
Add the oats and mix well.
Roll into balls about 1 inch in diameter.
Dip the balls into confectioners' sugar.
Place on wax paper and serve.

The "Girl Scouts Breakfast"

1 pound bacon
1 pound sausage
3 cans sliced potatoes
6-12 eggs
Salt and pepper
Instructions
First fry bacon and sausage until done. Drain the grease and add potatoes, while stirring constantly. Scramble eggs, and add to the meat and potatoes. Add salt and pepper if you want. You can also add onions, peppers, or other veggies too.

Not So Plain, Easy Potato's
8 cup mashed potatoes
4 strips bacon, diced
2 onions, thinly sliced
1 cup Parmesan cheese, grated
3 cloves of garlic, minced
2 tbsp. parsley, chopped
1 stick of butter
salt and pepper
Instructions
First boil a pot of water, and boil the potato's until cooked. Fry the bacon until crisp. Add onions and cook for five minutes, adding garlic near the end. Add bacon mixture and butter to potatoes, mixing thoroughly. Add seasonings as desired.

Chilli Rice

Serves 8
1 pound of ground beef
4 cup of rice
3 cups of water
1 cup chopped onions
1 large green pepper, chopped
Chili seasoning
1 can of tomatoes, undrained
1 can of drained kidney beans
1 tbsp. salt
1 cup shredded Cheddar cheese
Instructions
In a large frying pan, fry and drain beef. Add the remaining ingredients, except the cheese and stir. Bring to a boil. Cover and simmer for about 5 minutes. Sprinkle the cheese on top.

Campfire Steak

1 pound top sirloin steak
1/2 cup balsamic vinegar
1/4 cup olive oil
2 tsp. minced garlic
2 tbsp. honey or brown sugar
A dash of Worcestershire sauce
A dash of cayenne pepper

Instructions

Mix all ingredients in a sealable plastic container or Ziploc freezer bag. Let sit for at least 4 hours. Then toss the steak on the barbeque or campfire grill. Delicious! Wrap some potatoes in foil and cook in the fire as well.

Bbq Sandwiches

Serves 7
1 cup chopped celery
1/2 cup chopped onion
1/2 cup of ketchup
1/2 cup barbecue sauce
1/2 cup water
1 Tbsp. vinegar
1 Tbsp. Worcestershire sauce
1 Tbsp. brown sugar
1/2 tsp. chili powder
1/2 tsp. salt
1/4 tsp. pepper
1/4 tsp. garlic powder
2 pound(s) cooked and shredded beef brisket
6 -8 sandwich buns
Instructions
Combine all ingredients except for beef in a pot, and bring the sauce to a boil. Simmer the sauce for 5 minutes, and then add shredded beef. Simmer at least 20 minutes after adding beef. Serve on top of sandwich buns of your choice.

Fire Bbq Pita's

Serves 4
3/4 pound thinly sliced beef, cut in small strips
2/3 cup barbecue sauce
4 slices cheddar cheese
4 large pitas
Alfalfa sprouts
Tomato slices
Instructions
In a medium saucepan combine the beef and barbecue sauce. Cook over medium heat until the beef is cooked.
Place a cheese slice inside each pita. Spoon about 1/4 cup of the mixture into each pita. Each camper may add toppings of his or her choosing.

Beef In The Wild

2 pound(s) ground beef
24 oz. Steak Sauce
2 7 oz. cans of your favorite kind of mushrooms
Bread of your choosing
Instructions
Cook ground beef over fire in skillet until cooked. Add mushrooms and gravy. Serve over toast.

Beef Can Soup

1 pound ground beef
1 small onion, finely chopped
2 cans Minestrone soup
1 can of corn
1 can of beans

Instructions

Cook the ground beef in a pot. Drain. Cook onion in the pan. Add the beef back to the pan. Pour in soup, corn, and beans. Cook until hot. Taste before adding additional seasoning. Goes great with biscuits or cornbread!

No Taco Tacos

Corn Bread mix
2 pound(s) ground beef
2 packages taco seasoning
Instructions
Mix the corn bread mix as per directions on package and let stand. Cook ground beef, drain and add taco seasoning as per package directions. Put cornbread mix in ring around inside of a Dutch oven. Put the beef in center and use to push up corn bread as you go. Top with shredded taco cheese.

One Pot Dinner

3 chicken thighs
1 can beans, drained
1 can diced seasoned tomatoes
1 small onion
1 clove garlic

Instructions

Place the pot over the fire with the three chicken thighs on the bottom, followed by the beans, and the diced seasoned tomatoes. Chop the onions and garlic and add to the pot. After about 20 minutes you have a wonderful stew. For added flair you can add corn five minutes before serving.

Easy Mac N Cheese

8 oz. macaroni
8 oz. sour cream
2 cups cottage cheese
8 oz. cream cheese
1 small onion, chopped
salt and pepper
8 oz. cheddar cheese

Instructions
Line Dutch oven with two layers of Aluminum Foil. Prepare macaroni according to directions on package. Mix all ingredients together. Place over Dutch oven for 30 minutes or until cheese is melted and bubbly.

Mexican Casserole

Serves 8
2 pounds ground beef
2 packets of taco seasoning
2 cans of tomatoes
2 cups shredded cheese
2 cans beans
2 cans cream of mushroom soup
1 small can sliced black olives
2 green onions, diced
1 pickled jalapeno, sliced
1 package of 20 tortillas

Instructions

Cook ground beef over Dutch oven and drain. Mix everything but cheese, sliced jalapeno and tortillas. Heat and bring to a boil. Cut tortillas as needed into strips, layer with mixture, cheese and then tortillas, ending with cheese. Cover and bake for 30-45 minutes then uncover for 15 minutes and remove from fire and let stand for 5 minutes. Cut into squares.

Camping Stew

1 1/2 pounds ground beef
1 onion
2 cans of kidney beans
2-3 cans of stewed tomatoes
2 cans of sliced potatoes
2 bay leaves
Garlic
Worcestershire sauce
Salt and pepper

Instructions
In a pot, cook the meat and onions together. Add the bay leaves and Worcestershire sauce. Drain the beans and add to the pot. Add the tomatoes. Drain the potatoes and add them as well. Add Salt and pepper. Simmer until all the ingredients are hot. Ladle into bowls and serve with bread.

Smores In A Cone

1/2 cup miniature marshmallows
10 12x12-inch squares aluminum foil
1/2 cup milk chocolate chips
10 ice cream cones

Place 1 teaspoon chocolate chips into each ice cream cone, followed by a layer of mini marshmallows. Continue layering chips and marshmallows into the cone until full. Repeat with the remaining chips, marshmallows, and cones. Wrap each cone in aluminum foil.

Heat the cones over campfire until chocolate and marshmallows are melted, roughly 3 minutes.

Burritos

16 eggs
1 lb. of sausages
1 onion
2 cloves garlic, minced
6 potatoes, chopped
2 cups cheddar cheese, shredded
4 green onions, chopped
3 tsp. parsley, chopped
8 tortillas
salt and pepper
Tin Foil
Salsa or hot sauce
Instructions
Chop potatoes and boil in a pot until soft.Chop the green onions and set aside.Crack 16 eggs and cook over low heat until you have scrambled eggs.Add salt and pepper.Sauté onions and garlic in 2 tsp. of olive oil.Add sausage to onion mixture and cook.In a large bowl combine sausage mixture, scrambled eggs, potatoes, cheese, green onions, parsley, and salt and pepper.Split the ingredients into 8 tortilla shells.Roll and wrap in tin foil and throw on the fire!

Dutch Oven Potato's

Potatoes
Bacon
Cheese
Onions
Salt and pepper
Instructions

Slice the potatoes and onions. Chop the bacon and add it to your warm Dutch oven. Spoon out the cooked bacon. Leave the grease in the bottom of the pan.

Now layer the ingredients:

First potatoes, salt and pepper, onions, cheese and bacon. Repeat layers and cook for 45 minutes or until the potatoes are soft.

Pizza Nachos

Sauce Ingredients
1-½ tbsp. unsalted butter
½ tbsp. olive oil
3 cloves garlic, minced
½ cup cream
¼ cup milk
A pinch of salt
A pinch of red pepper flakes
¼ cups Parmesan Cheese, Grated

Nacho Ingredients
1 bag of tortilla chips
¼ cup of onions, chopped
½ cup of pepperoni, cubed
½ cup of black olives, sliced
½ green bell pepper, diced
1 cup cheddar cheese, shredded

Instructions
Melt butter in a pan. Add the parmesan cheese to the melted butter and blend. Add in cream and milk, stir until blended. Add in remaining ingredients for the sauce. Simmer on low, do not let it boil. Layer the chips on an oven safe pan. Pour sauce over the chips and layer the remaining nacho ingredients. Heat in the oven at 350°F until cheese is melted. Remove from oven and serve.

Campfire Éclairs

crescent rolls
snack pack pudding
chocolate frosting
whip cream
wooden dowels
oil of your choosing (vegetable, olive, canola)
Instructions
Take a wooden dowel and coat the cooking end with oil. Wrap crescent rolls around the top and push about 3-4" down the wooden dowel. Make sure it doesn't have any holes. Cook over fire until golden brown. Remove from dowel and add your favorite pudding to the inside. Frost the tops and add whip cream.

Kabobs In A Bag

Chicken Or Beef

Peppers
Mushrooms
1 onion
Jalapeno peppers
Potatoes
Garlic
3 tbsp. olive oil
Lemon juice
Chicken seasoning
Butter flavoring
2 tbsp. of soy sauce
Lemon pepper seasoning
Dill seasoning
Instructions

Start by boiling potatoes for around 5 minutes depending on size of potato. Do not cook until mushy they must still be firm. Let potatoes cool completely (they will cook again on grill) . Chop peppers and the onion. Put chopped vegetables, jalapenos, potatoes and mushrooms into a foil bag along with the garlic, olive oil, lemon juice, soy sauce, butter flavoring, lemon pepper seasoning, and dill seasoning. Cut meat into medium size pieces. Place meat in a different foil bag with ¼ cup of olive oil, garlic, chicken seasonings, butter flavoring and 2 tbsp. of soy sauce. Place the foil bags into larger zip lock bag for storage while traveling. To cook, remove from foil bags and grill for roughly 10 minutes, turning every 2 minutes. Let cool before opening foil bags.

Conclusion

Thank you again for downloading this book!

I hope this book was able to help you to get delicious camping meal ideas.

The next step is to take action and prepare these meals to your family while you're spending a great trip together.

Thank you and good luck!

Part 2

Campfire Cooking

A "Girl Scouts" Breakfast

Ingredients
1 pound(s)bacon
1 pound(s)sausage
3-4cans sliced potatoes
8 - 12eggs
salt and pepper
Directions
Fry bacon and sausage together until done. Drain grease. Add potatoes, stirring constantly to keep from sticking. Scramble eggs, then add to the meat and potatoes. Salt and pepper to taste. You can add onions, peppers, or other veggies too.

All In One Potato Frittata

Makes: 4
Ingredients
1 medium potato (peel and dice)
8 eggs
1/2 c milk
1/2 tsp dried basil
1/2 tsp salt
pepper to taste
2 Tbsp oil
medium onion (chopped)
1/2 green pepper (diced)
1/2 red pepper (diced)
1 small zucchini diced
1 clove garlic minced
1/2 c shredded cheddar cheese
Directions
1 Cook potato in salted boiling water until tender. Drain. Beat together eggs, milk, basil, salt and pepper until eggs are just blended. In a 10 inch ovenproof skillet, heat oil over medium heat. Add onion, peppers and/or zucchini & garlic. Sauté 3 minutes. Add potato and sauté 2 minutes longer. Pour eggs over vegetables in skillet. Cook over low to medium heat until eggs are almost set, but still moist on the surface [10-12 minutes] occasionally lift edge of the eggs to allow uncooked egg to run to bottom of skillet. Sprinkle top with cheese. Place under broiler until cheese melts, 2-3 minutes. Cut into wedges to serve. If no broiler is available, still sprinkle cheese on, it will melt. Serve with crusty roll & salad.

Apple Pie On A Stick

Ingredients
1 c sugar
1 Tbsp cinnamon
4 cooking apples
4 dowel or roasting sticks

Directions

In a small bowl, mix together sugar and cinnamon and set aside. Push the stick or dowel through the top of the apple to the bottom until the apple is secure. Roast the apple 2 to 3 inches above the bed of hot coals and turn frequently. (As the apple cooks, the skin starts to brown and the juice dribbles out.) When the skin is loose, remove the apple from the coals but leave it on the stick. Peel the skin off the apple, being careful not to burn yourself because the apple is very hot.

Baby Red Potatoes

Makes: 6
Ingredients
Approximately 20 baby red potatoes
1 packet dry Italian dressing mix
Olive oil
Directions
Cut potatoes into bite-sized pieces. Place in a large bowl, toss with Olive oil until lightly coated. Sprinkle dressing mix over potatoes and toss until all sides are covered. Wrap in foil, put near coals or on BBQ grill until potatoes are fork tender. Potatoes can also be cooked spread in a baking sheet and put in over for 45 minutes at 350 degrees.

Backwoods Chili Rice Skillet

Ingredients
1 pound(s)ground beef
4cUncle Ben's Quick brand rice
3 cwater
1 cchopped onion
1 large green pepper, chopped
1 package chili seasoning mix
1 can tomatoes, undrained
1 can kidney beans, drained
1 Tbspsalt
1 cshredded Cheddar or Monterey Jack cheese

Directions
In a large skillet, brown meat, drain. Add remaining ingredients except cheese; stir. Bring to a vigorous boil. Cover tightly. Simmer about 5 minutes or until desired consistency. Sprinkle with cheese.

Bacon & Cheddar Grilled Cheese Sandwich

Makes: 1
Ingredients
bread (we like raisin bread)
bacon (we use leftover bacon from breakfast)
cheddar cheese
olive oil spray
Directions
Place bacon and cheese between slices of bread. Spray cooking surface with oilive oil and toast on a skillet over an RV stove or in a Coleman sandwich toaster over the fire.

Bag Kabobs

Ingredients
beef or chicken
bell peppers
mushrooms
onion
jalapeno peppers (optional)
small potatoes
zucchini squash
fresh garlic
2-3Tbsp olive oil
lemon or lime
McCormick's Salt-free Chicken seasoning
powdered butter flavoring
2Tbsp soy sauce
lemon pepper seasonings
dill

Directions

Boil potatoes for approximately 4-5 minutes depending on size. They should still be firm and crisp, not mushy. They will finish cooking on the grill. Let potatoes cool completely before putting in foil bag. Chop bell peppers, onion and zucchini squash into large pieces. Put chopped vegetables, whole jalapenos, whole potatoes and whole mushrooms into a large foil bag with garlic, olive oil, lemon or lime juice, soy sauce, butter flavoring, lemon pepper seasonings, and dill. Cut meat into large stew size pieces. Put meat in a separate foil bag with 1/4 cup of olive oil, garlic, chicken seasonings, butter flavoring and 2 tablespoons of soy sauce. When using more than one kind of meat, put in separate bags. Place the foil bags into larger 2 gallon ziplock bags to store while traveling. To cook, remove foil bags from plastic ziplock bags and grill for 8-10 minutes, turning after 5-6 minutes. Let sit before opening bags.

Baked Apples

Ingredients
Granny Smith Apples
butter
brown sugar
cinnamon candies
caramels
Directions
Use as many Granny Smith Apples as you need for your camping crowd. Core the apple, leaving a thin layer on the bottom. In the cored out area, put a pat of butter and about a tablespoon of brown sugar. This will depend on how big your apples are, remember the brown sugar will melt down into the butter. The rest is up to you, you can put in a few cinnamon candies, or a couple carmels, depending on the flavor you like. Wrap the apples in foil, (if your coals are hot, double wrap, if they are cooler, single wrap). The apples are placed on the coals, and rolled evey 10 minutes or so. They usually take about a half hour, depending again upon the heat of your coals. If you are lucky enough to have a freezer, you could add ice cream when you serve these. We have also served them with a whipped topping, cheese, or if your a purist...just as they come from the fire.

Baked Onions

Ingredients
onion per person
black pepper
butter or margarine
Directions
Take an onion and take off outer skin. Hollow out the core and add cracked fresh ground black pepper and put a large pat of butter or margarine in the hole. Wrap in aluminum foil and bake on grill for about an hour on medium, or in oven at 325 degrees for an hour. The onion is juicy, sweet and delicious.

Baked Pancakes

Ingredients
1 pound(s)sausage
6eggs
1 c milk
1 c self rising flour
1 tspvanilla
1 stick margarine
Directions
Begin by browning the sausage. While sausage is browning, in bowl mix six eggs, 1 cup milk, and one cup self rising flour and 1 tsp. vanilla. Mix together well. In 13 X 9 pan melt one stick margarine and pour in cooked sausage. Pour the batter on top of the sausage. Cook at 400 degrees about 20 minutes or until golden brown. Serve with syrup or ketchup, my family has tried it with both.

Baked Potato In A Can

Ingredients
1 medium size potato
butter
salt
pepper
heavy duty aluminum foil
tin can (from veggies or beans)

Directions
Clean the potato. Butter the outside of the potato really well, and season to taste. Put potato into the tin can and cover top of can with foil. Place the tin can next to a fire pit of coals and let it set for 25 minutes, then turn can 90° and cook for another 20 minutes (do not peek at potato). After 45 minutes you will have a perfect baked potato.

Balsamic Steak

Ingredients
1 pound(s) top sirloin steak
1/2 c balsamic vinegar
1/4 c olive oil
1-2 tsp minced garlic
2 Tbsp honey or brown sugar
dash Worcestershire sauce
salt and pepper
dash cayenne pepper

Directions
Mix all ingredients in a sealable plastic container or Ziploc freezer bag. Let sit for at least 4 hours. Then toss the steak on the barbeque or campfire grill. Delicious! Wrap some potatoes in foil and cook in the fire as well.

Balsamic Vinegar Chicken

Ingredients
4boneless, skinless chicken breast halves
3/4cbalsamic vinegar
Directions
Place the chicken and balsamic vinegar in a zip-top bag. Squeeze out as much of the air as possible when sealing. Place in refrigerator and marinate 4-12 hours (longer is better). Remove chicken from marinade and discard remaining liquid. The dark color of the vinegar will make the chicken appear almost brownish-gray. Don't worry - it'll be fine. Place chicken on grill over medium heat or you can pan fry covered over medium heat adding water to cover bottom of pan. Cook until no longer pink in center and juices run clear.

This goes well with rice, pasta or bread and a salad. Leftovers are great chunked into a big fresh salad with a light vinegarette dressing.

Banana Boat

Ingredients
1 banana
1/2 milk chocolate bar
3-5 marshmellows (full size)
aluminum foil
Directions
Cut the banana in half, lengthwise. Top the bottom half of the banana with the chocolate and marshmellows, then replace the top half, sandwiching the ingredients between the banana slices. Wrap in aluminum foil and heat- either over open fire, on a grill, or on the RV stove. Unwrap and enjoy!

Banana Boats

Ingredients
Bananas
Chocolate Bars
Marshmallows
Directions
Peel a banana back but don't pull the peel completely off. Slice it longways so it looks like a hot dog bun. Put marshmallows, chocolate bar pieces, and chocolate syrup in the sliced area. Then wrap the banana back up in its peel. Then wrap the banana in foil and put in the hot coals. Leave for about 10 minutes. Unwrap the foil and the banana peel and enjoy. The banana is so soft, along with the melted marshmallows and chocolate.

You can also do variations with carmel syrup, strawberries, peanut butter. Anything that tastes good with bananas works great. We try all kinds of combinations.

Banana Chocolate Chip Split

Ingredients
1 banana
1 1/2 Tbsp semi-sweet chocolate chips
1 1/2 Tbsp mini marshmallows
Directions
With peel left on slice banana lengthwise across top of banana (do not cut through). Spread top of banana slightly open and fill with marshmallows and chocolate chips. Squeeze banana closed as much as possible and wrap tightly in tinfoil (shiny side in). Lay tin foil wrapped banana on campfire grate for approx. 10 minutes. Carefully remove banana from fire and open the tin foil just enough to get a spoon inside.

Bar-B-Que Bean Bake

Ingredients
1 pound(s)ground beef
1 pound(s)bacon
1 large onion, chopped
4Tbspmustard
4Tbspmolasses or 1/2 cup brown sugar
3/4tsppepper
2 16 oz. cans red kidney beans, with juice
2 16 oz. cans pork & beans, with juice
16 oz. cans butter beans, drained
1/2cketchup
1/2cbar-b-que sauce
1 tspsalt
1 tspchili powder

Directions
Cook bacon, drain and chop. Cook beef and onion. Drain off fat. Mix all of the above ingredients together well. Simmer for 30 minutes stirring occasionally or put in Dutch oven and place on hot coals for 45 minutes, stirring occasionally. (At home, bake 1 hour at 350 degrees). Cut recipe in half for smaller family dish.

Bbq Pitas

Makes: 4

Ingredients

3/4 pound(s) thinly sliced beef or pork from the deli, cut in 1/2 inch strips

2/3 c barbecue sauce

4 thin slices smoked cheddar, Swiss, or Monterey Jack cheese with jalapeno peppers from the deli, cut in half

4 large pita bread rounds, split crosswise to form pockets

alfalfa sprouts, tomato slices and/or sliced dill pickles

Directions

In a medium saucepan combine meat and barbecue sauce. Cook, covered, over medium heat till heated through, stirring occasionally.

Place a cheese slice half inside each pita bread half. Spoon about 1/4 cup of the meat mixture into each pita bread half. Have each camper add the toppers they choose for a personalized pita dinner.

Bbq Potato Chips

Ingredients
potatoes, cut into slices
olive oil
Mrs. Dash seasoning
Directions
Slice potatoes 1/4" thick. Lay them on a plate, brush one side with olive oil. Season to taste. I like Mrs. Dash and throw them on the hot grill, oiled side down. Brush the other side with oil, and season. Turn them after about 3 minutes and grill another 3 - 4 minutes.

Bbq Ribs

Ingredients
1/2c brown sugar
1/2c apple butter
1/4c bourbon
1/4c cider vinegar
1/4c apple cider
2 Tbsp Dijon mustard
Rub:
1-2 teaspoons of salt (Kosher is better)
½ cup apple butter (apple sauce can be substituted but not as good)
1 tablespoon of brown sugar
2 tsp dry mustard
2 tsp thyme
1 tsp ground ginger
½ tsp cinnamon
½ tsp cayenne pepper
1 Sliced onion
2 tablespoons ginger
1 tsp cinnamon
1 ½ cups apple cider
Directions
Always remove membrane from the back of the ribs. Mix rub ingredients together and rub all over both sides of ribs. Let rub do its magic for 4 hours or more in the refrigerator. Put onion, ginger, cinnamon & apple cider in large roasting pan and mix until evenly distributed place ribs in roasting pan. Cover with foil and cook over medium heat for 2 hours. While ribs are cooking in roasting pan, mix BBQ sauce, grill ribs over indirect medium heat for an additional hour brushing BBQ sauce on lightly every 15 minutes. Use smoking chips at this point if you like (sweeter chips are better). When ribs are done, cover with plastic wrap for ½ hour before serving. While ribs are cooling in a covered pan,

take remaining BBQ sauce and a ½ cup of the roasting sauce and bring to a boil and let simmer until fairly thick. When done, serve on the side. Use a charcoal grill with a lid or over a fire. These are simply the best sweet ribs you ever tasted.

Beef In The Wild

Ingredients
2pound(s)ground beef
46 oz. cans Dawn Fresh Mushroom Steak Sauce
27 oz. cans pieces and stems mushrooms (drained)
toasted bread
Directions
Cook ground beef over fire in skillet until no longer pink. Add the mushrooms and gravy and combine. Serve over toast. Easy, hearty, inexpensive, and delicious. Kids love it.

Berry Pie

Ingredients
4c berries (strawberries, blueberries or raspberries)
milk
6 Bisquick or biscuit dough
dash brown sugar
cream or whipped cream

Directions
Take your favorite berries, wash them and if you are using large berries, like strawberries, you will want to cut them into smaller pieces. Find your trusty camp pot with lid and fill the bottom with the berries. Then take your bisquick and mix enough dough to make about 6 biscuits/dumplings (usually about half the suggested recipe on the box). Then drop dumplings into the pot, making about 5-6 round lumps with small spaces between for air to escape. Then fill the pot with milk, just until the milk is barely at the top of the dumplings or if the berries are frozen, use less milk. Do NOT completely cover the dumplings or you'll end up with mush. Cover pot tightly with lid. Put on medium to low heat for about 20 minutes or until the milk has been absorbed and dumplings are light and fluffy. Be careful not to burn the berries on the bottom. Serve warm or cold with a little cream and sprinkled with brown sugar. After picking fresh berries, what a sweet reward!

Big Jim's Camping Beans

Ingredients
1 pound(s)bulk breakfast sausage (crumbled and cooked)
1 pound(s)ground beef (crumbled and cooked)
1 large onion
1 bell pepper
2 jalepeno peppers
1 can butter beans
1 can kidney beans
1 can green beans
1/2cK.C. Masterpiece BBQ sauce
3 Tbspdark brown sugar
Directions
Dice and sauté onion, bell pepper and jalepeno pepper with meat. In either a crock pot or baking dish, add beans, BBQ sauce and brown sugar. Cook in crock pot on high until thoroughly heated thru or in an oven at 375 degrees for 45 minutes. Serve and enjoy as side dish or main dish.

Biscuits On A Stick

Ingredients
Ready to bake biscuits
Directions
Because you are cooking a biscuit, you can't use a small stick or cloths-hanger. You will need to have a stick that is about ¾ of an inch to 1 in diameter. (Dowel rods work real good, but you can use anything, I usually cut up some scrap wood that I always have around the house). Once you get your sticks, you need to put tin foil around the end of the stick covering a good six inches. If you don't do this your stick will probably start burning, which sort of takes the fun out of cooking the biscuit.

You also need a can of biscuits, you know the kind that pops open and you just put them on a cookie sheet. I think any type of biscuit would work, just regular or large biscuits. Insert the foil covered stick into the biscuit and roast over a campfire until golden brown on the outside and baked completely on the inside.

Blair's Campfire Stew

Ingredients
1 pound(s)sirloin
4red potatoes
1 red onion
1-2cvegetables
1 tspsalt
1 tspground black pepper
3 Tbspbutter
Directions
Preheat your grill to medium heat. Measure out 2 or 3 sheets of aluminum foil in 2-foot lengths, and layer one on top of the other (or a large aluminum grilling bag is easier). Layer the meat (cut in small chunks), sliced potatoes and onion and vegetables in the center, sprinkle with salt and pepper, and dot with butter. Wrap into a flattened square and seal the edges. Place aluminum wrapped package over medium heat and cover. Cook for approximately 40 minutes, turning once. Serve hot right off the grill.

Blondies

Ingredients
1 1/2c self-rising flour
1 1/2 sticks unsalted butter
1 1/2c packed brown sugar
2 large eggs
1 1/2 tsp vanilla extract
1/2c semisweet chocolate chips
1/2c white chocolate chips
1 c pecans (toasted)

Directions
Line 12" Dutch oven with foil and spray with non-stick baking oil. Whisk the butter and brown sugar until combined. Add eggs and vanilla, mix well. Fold in flour until just combined, Do not overmix. Fold in chocolate chips and nuts - turn batter into the prepared pot. Bake until the top is shiny and cracked - feels firm to touch. About 20 minutes over medium heat, then remove and add top coals for final baking - approximately 10 minutes. Cool completely before cutting into about 24 servings.

Bratwurts & Swiss

Ingredients
Italian sausage or Johnson's Bratwursts and cheese
your favorite cheese slices
Directions
Place Italian Sausage/Johnson's Bratwursts on a stick and cook over the fire (be sure to turn often) until thoroughly cooked. Place in hot dog bun and cover with a slice of your favorite cheese (I prefer Swiss cheese) YUM YUM - Eat on the go or on your plate with a few chips for a fast meal.

Breakfast Bag

Ingredients
1 - 2slice(s)bacon
1 cFrozen hashbrowns, thawed
1 - 2eggs
brown paper bag

Directions

Build a simmering campfire. In a lunch-sized brown paper bag, place bacon slices and thawed hash browns. Crack eggs into bag. Fold paper bag down, leaving 3" of space above food. Insert a pointed stick through the folded part of the bag. Hold stick so bag hangs about 4" to 5" above hot coals. Cook for about 8 to 10 minutes, being careful not to let the bag catch on fire.

Remove bag from heat and, using an oven mitt, fold open to check that eggs have been cooked throughout. If eggs have not completely cooked, refold paper bag and hold over hot coals for an additional 2 to 3 minutes. Fold down paper bag and eat breakfast directly from bag.

Breakfast Burrito

Ingredients
eggs
hash browns
bacon
cheddar cheese
salsa
flour tortilla shells
sour cream
tomatoes
olives
green onions
avocado

Directions

Ahead of time you can chop up the tomatoes, olives, green onions and avocado. Cook the bacon and crumble. Cook the southern style hash browns in a frying pan with salt, pepper and oil until browned. Mix together and put in a container or zip lock bag and refrigerate until needed. Grate cheddar cheese (store in container or zip lock bag). On the morning you will cook these, take out mixture and place in large frying pan and heat. Scramble the eggs, add to warm mixture and cook. This is an ideal way to have breakfast while camping because each person can make their own burrito the way they like it.

Breakfast Burritos With Sausage

Ingredients
2pound(s)Jimmy Dean or your favorite breakfast sausage
24eggs
1 - 2pound(s)package shredded cheddar cheese
20large flour tortillas
Directions
Cook breakfast sausage and scramble the eggs. Preheat a few tortillas in your microwave at home, spoon out generous portions of sausage, scrambled eggs & cheese on a softened tortilla and roll it up. Wrap it individually in aluminum foil. You can then freeze them if you would like, they keep well.

To cook, place them on a grill surface over the camp fire. Look for the tortilla to be slightly brown and crispy. Put some hot sauce on it and its a breakfast fit for a king.

Brown Bears

Ingredients
1/2c sugar
1/2 Tbsp cinnamon
4 Tbsp butter (melted)
1 package bread dough
Directions
Mix sugar & cinnamon together until well blended. Melt butter in shallow pan, such as a round cake pan. Take the biscuits and roll in hands to form snake shaped pieces. Wrap the snake-like dough around a stick in a coil fashion. Cook over a campfire until evenly browned. Roll the cooked dough in the melted butter and then in the cinnamon/sugar mixture. Yum.

Brunswick Stew

Make: 12 - 14

Ingredients
3 large smoked ham hocks (sliced 1" thick)
3 pound(s)stewing chicken (cut up)
2pound(s)beef stew meat
2bay leaves
1 tspthyme, parsley
3 stalks celery
2 onions (cut in wedges)
1 Tbspblack peppercorns
2 TbspDurkee Six-Pepper Blend
2 cans tomatoes (cut up)
2ccarrots (peeled and chopped)
2ccelery (chopped)
2conions (chopped)
3 large potatoes (diced)
2clima beans (frozen)
3 ccorn (fresh off the cob)

Directions

Add ham hocks, chicken and beef stew meat to 14" deep or 16" Dutch oven. Add bay leaves, thyme, parsley, celery stalks, onion wedges, Six-Pepper Blend and peppercorns. Simmer covered until chicken and beef are thoroughly tender, about 2 hours. Remove meat and set aside to cool. Strain the stock and discard veggies and herbs. Skim off some of the fat. Add tomatoes, carrots, chopped celery, onions, potatoes, lima beans and corn to strained stock. Simmer uncovered until all vegetables are tender, about 30 to 45 minutes. Bone chicken and remove pieces of ham hock from the bone. Return meat to pot. Add more water if needed to make more soup. Simmer for 10 to 15 minutes and season with salt and pepper. Serve with cornbread and enjoy!

Buger & Veggie Pouches

Ingredients
4 hamburger patties
1 onion (sliced)
1 can mushroom soup
potatoes
squash
butter
seasoning to taste
Directions
Place hamburger patties on foil. Cover with a layer of onions and mushroom soup. Fold foil into pouch. On a second piece of foil, slice potatoes 1/2 inch thick and alternate layers with onions topping with a few slices of butter and your choice of seasoning. Slice squash and add to potatoes. Wrap up foil. Throw it all on the Webber or camp fire. Wait one hour turning every 15 minutes.

Cajun Shrimp Gumbo

Ingredients
1 onion
1 green pepper
2 cloves garlic
1/4c butter
corn (32 ounces frozen or 1 can)
1 can Rotel Diced Tomatoes & Green Chilies
1 Tbsp sugar
1 tsp salt
1/4tsp pepper
dash cayenne pepper
1/2 large can canned milk (make sure to use canned milk)
1/4c chopped green onions
2 pound(s) shrimp (shelled or canned or frozen)
corn starch

Directions
Chop the onion, green pepper and garlic cloves. Sauté onion, pepper & garlic in butter to a tender crisp. Add corn, tomatoes, sugar, and salt & pepper and heat for 10 minutes. Add canned milk and green onions and heat 4-5 minutes. Add shrimp at the right time, (adjust the time if using raw or cooked shrimp), you do not want to over cook the shrimp. Make a paste using the cornstarch and some water to thicken. Serve over Rice. If you don't like spicy, use Rotel mild diced tomatoes & green chilies and cut back on the Cayenne. This recipe is very versatile because you can use canned corn, canned shrimp and you can prepare the veggies at home.

Camp Beef Brisket

Makes: 10

Ingredients
1/4 c paprika
2 Tbsp garlic, minced
1 Tbsp thyme
1 Tbsp basil
1 Tbsp oregano
1 Tbsp dried parsley
1 Tbsp ground black pepper
1/2 tsp cayenne
1/2 tsp ground nutmeg
2 Tbsp Tabasco sauce
2 Tbsp Worcestershire sauce
3-4 pound(s) beef brisket

Directions

Mix all the spices together, then dry rub the meat. Coat with Tabasco and Worcestershire sauce, rubbing in carefully not to displace spices. Refrigerate for 3 to 5 days - if time permits. Place meat trivet in bottom of Dutch oven large enough to hold brisket. Place brisket (fat side up) on trivet. Cover and hang low over the fire to get the pot hot. When the meat starts to sizzle, raise to the highest hook and cook over low fire for approximately 12 hours. Go for a ride, take a nap, do some fishing and cook the brisket overnight. Low and slow is the key to a good, juicy brisket that is fork tender, and that's just all there is to it! When it's done, throw it on the grill to crispy the outside, slice and pour the juices from the pot over the meat.

Camp Bread

Ingredients
1 16 oz. package hot roll mix
1 Tbsp snipped fresh rosemary or basil or 1 Tsp. dried rosemary or basil, crushed
1/2 cs shredded Parmesan cheese
cornmeal

Directions
Prepare hot roll mix in a 10-inch Dutch oven according to package directions, adding the rosemary or basil and 1/4 cup of the Parmesan cheese to the dry ingredients (omit kneading step). Remove dough.

Grease the Dutch oven and sprinkle with cornmeal. Place dough in Dutch oven. Using greased hands, gently press dough evenly into the bottom of Dutch oven. If desired, use a small knife to make a decorative pattern on top of the bread. Sprinkle with remaining 1/4 cup Parmesan cheese. Cover and let rise in a warm place until dough nearly doubles (30 to 40 minutes).

Cover Dutch oven and arrange 8 to 10 hot coals around the edge of the Dutch oven and 10 to 12 hot coals on the lid. Bake for 20 to 25 minutes or until golden, rotating the Dutch oven a half-turn halfway through cooking. Makes 12 servings.

Camp Eclairs

Ingredients
1 can of biscuit dough
vanilla pudding
chocolate frosting
Directions
Take the biscuit dough and mold 1-2 biscuits together. Get a stick about 3/4" to 1" in diameter and mold the dough around the stick so it is about 6 inches long and the dough totally surrounds the stick. Toast the dough over the campfire until it gets golden brown on the outside. When the dough turns golden brown, slide it off the end of the stick, (this will leave a hole going through the center). Fill this hole (where the stick was) with vanilla pudding and top with the chocolate frosting.

Camp Fruit Cobbler

Ingredients
2-4cans fruit pie filling
1-2cans refrigerated biscuits or 1 recipe bisquick biscuit dough
1/4-1/3cbrown sugar
1-2Tbspcinnamon
Directions
Burn campfire down to very hot coals. Spray dutch oven with cooking spray. Add fruit pie filling (i'ts sometimes a real treat to mix flavors). Cover with refrigerated biscuits or biscuit dough. Sprinkle with brown sugar and cinnamon. Cover and place in center of coals with coals coming up around the sides. With your handy shovel, cover lid with coals as well. Cobbler is done when biscuits are golden brown. Check after 15 minutes and then every 5-7 minutes after that until done. Enjoy!

Camp Stew

Ingredients
2 pound(s) hamburger
1 can stewed tomatos
1 can corn
1 c elbow macaroni
1/2 c chopped onions
1 c water
1/4 pound(s) cheddar cheese
Directions
Brown hamburger in dutch oven, kettle, or skillet. Drain. Stir in tomatoes, corn, macaroni, and water. Cook until hot. Just before serving add cheese.

Camp Stove Goulash

Ingredients
1 pound(s)ground meat (turkey, beef or chicken)
1 sweet onion
1 green or red pepper
1 16 ounce can diced tomatoes (Mexican flavor)
1 16 ounce can garbanzo beans
1 can corn
ketchup (optional)
rice

Directions
Brown the beef, onions and pepper in large skillet or pan. Chop up the onion and green or red pepper. Add the tomatoes, garbanzo beans (drained), corn and a squirt of ketchup (if desired) and serve over rice (Our favorite is the boil in the bag kind).

Camp Taters

Ingredients
4potatoes
1 red bell pepper
1 green bell pepper
1 onion
salt and pepper
1/4stick of butter
Directions
Slice poatoes in 1/4 inch horizontal slices. Slice 1/2 of red and 1/2 of green peppers lengthwise in thin strips, slice 1/2 onion in small strips. Melt butter and mix all ingredients in large bowl. Season to taste, wrap in double foil and grill until brown on both sides.

Camper's Luau Chicken

Makes: 2

Ingredients

3 envelopes onion cup-a-soup
8 oz. can crushed pineapple, undrained
1 whole chicken breast, split
1 small green bell pepper, cut into strips
2 18-inch square pieces heavy-duty aluminum foil

Directions

In a small bowl, combine onion cup-a-soup and pineapple.

For each serving, place half the chicken, onion-pineapple mixture and green pepper on foil. Wrap loosely, sealing edges airtight with double fold. Place on grill, seam-side up, over hot coals or high heat, and cook 45 minutes, or until chicken is tender.

Camper's Pizza Skillet Delight

Ingredients
1 pound(s)ground beef
1 can (4 oz.) sliced mushrooms
water
1 can (8 oz.) pizza sauce
3 cUncle Ben's Quick Brand Rice
1 large green pepper, chopped
1 1/2tspsalt
1 tsporegano
1/4cgrated Parmesan cheese
6thin slices Mozzarella cheese

Directions
Brown meat in a 10-inch skillet; drain. Drain mushrooms, reserving juice. Add water to juice to make 2 cups liquid. Add liquid, pizza sauce, rice, mushrooms, green pepper, salt and oregano to beef; stir. Bring to boil. Reduce heat, cover and simmer until liquid is absorbed, about 5 minutes. Sprinkle Parmesan and arrange Mozzarella on top of beef-rice mixture. Cover skillet and heat for 2-3 minutes, or until cheese softens.

Camper's Skillet

Ingredients
4large potatoes, diced or sliced
6large eggs or egg beaters
6 - 8sausage links
1 medium sized onion, chopped
1 green pepper,chopped
seasoning salt
Directions
Fry sausages, cubed potatoes, chopped onions & green peppers. Season salt to taste. Break eggs or pour egg beaters over skillet contents. Mix until eggs are done.

Campers Stew

Ingredients
hamburger patty
onion (sliced)
white potatoes (sliced)
sweet potatoes (sliced)
baby carrots
1 Tbspbutter
salt & pepper to taste
Directions
Place in foil pouch. Put on Grill or in Oven or even over a campfire for about 40-45 minutes or until burger is done and vegetables are tender.

Campfire Chicken & Vegetables

Ingredients
2boneless, skinless chicken breasts
1 bag baby carrots
onions
potatoes
1 cream of chicken soup
Directions
You will need heavy duty aluminum foil. Get your coals really hot and fire red. While they are heating, prepare your chicken. Tear off foil big enough to hold chicken and large vegetables. Place chicken breasts on foil and add 1/2 the can of soup. Cube the potatoes and onions. Place cut up potatoes, onion and your carrots on top of the chicken. Fold foil tightly, be sure to seal so the soup doesn't leak out. Place on fire grate or directly on hot coals. Cook for approximately 30 minutes, turning at least once.

Campfire Chicken & Veggies

Ingredients
boneless skinless chicken breast
red potatoes
baby carrots
green peppers
onion
corn
italian dressing (or spice mixture of your choice)
Directions
You will need Reynolds foil grill bags. Cut everything up, put it in a bag, and cover it with italian dressing (usually about half a bottle per foil bag), roll the bag down, throw the grate over the campfire or directly on hot coals. Cook until potatoes are tender and chicken is cooked. ENJOY!!!

Campfire Chicken Pot Pie

Ingredients
4-6 Whole Boneless Chicken Breast (or chicken of choice)
1 Cream of Chicken, Mushroom or Broccoli Soup
1/2c water or milk
1 Can Mushrooms
2 Bags of Califlower, Broccoli and Carrots (frozen vegetable mix)
1 large onion
Olive Oil
Butter
Salt & Pepper (or seasoning of choice)
Cooking Spray

Directions
pray the bottom of a medium sized foil baking pan with the cooking spray. Line the bottom of the pan with sliced onions. Spread the sliced mushrooms and frozen vegetable mix over the onion layer. Mix soup and water (or milk). Spread soup mixture over vegetables. Add a little olive oil and butter. Season chicken and place on top of mixture. Using heavy duty aluminum foil, cover the pan completely from side to side and end to end wrapping all the way over the bottom of the pan to create a good seal. Put on camping rack over hot coals. Check for doneness after approximately 1 hour (cooking time will vary depending on the heat from the coals). You may place directly on the coals, but the mixture may stick to the bottom of the pan. Serve with your choice of bread.

Campfire Chili With Hamburger

Makes: 5
Ingredients
1-1/2 pound(s) hamburger
1 onion, chopped
1 clove minced garlic
1 14.5 oz. can stewed tomatos
1 16 oz. can pinto beans
1 8 oz. can tomato sauce
1 c ketchup
2 c water
4 tsp chili powder
1 tsp cumin
1 Tbsp sugar
1/2 green pepper, chopped
1/2 jalapeno, diced without seeds
salt and pepper to taste
Directions
Cook hamburger, onions and garlic together over medium high heat until hamburger is cooked thoroughly. Then add remaining ingredients in the order listed above and mix. Simmer chili over medium low heat for 15 to 20 minutes and serve.

Campfire Chili

Ingredients
1 can hot chili red beans
1 can chili seasoned chopped tomatoes
1 can tomato sauce
1 small can tomato paste
1 can tomato juice
2 pound(s)hamburger
1 onion
1 small carrot
1 small potato
chili powder
tabasco sauce
Directions
Shred the carrot and the potato. Add chili powder and Tabasco sauce to taste. Brown hamburger, then add the rest of the ingredients. Cook over fire embers for at least 4 to 6 hours with a light boil. Serve and Enjoy!

Campfire Corn

Ingredients
corn on the cob
2 Tbsp butter
salt and pepper
Directions
Rub butter on each corn cob and salt & pepper, then wrap each individual cob in aluminum foil. Place on BBQ grill.

Campfire Delights

Ingredients
peanut butter
1-2 bananas
2 Hershey bars
1 bag of marshmallows
2 slice(s) bread

Directions
On a piece of bread spread peanut butter, place 4-5 slices of banana, 2-3 small chocolate squares, and 2-3 marshmallows. Cover with another piece of bread and place in a greased pie iron. Cook over a campfire until bread is golden brown. Enjoy!

Campfire Dessert Wraps

Ingredients
flour tortilla for each person
peanut butter
mini-marshmallows
mini-chocolate chips
Directions
Spread each tortilla with peanut butter. Put on marshmallows and chocolate chips. Amount varies with each person's taste and size of tortilla. Roll like a burrito. Wrap in foil and warm on the grill or the campfire for about 15 minutes. Handle with oven mitts or pot holders or towels, since they will be hot! Peel and eat like a banana!! Delicious! Can add toffee bits, fruit, sprinkles or use caramel topping instead of peanut butter or add or eliminate an ingredient! Your imagination and ability to roll is your only limit. Have tried these in the oven and they are okay, but we prefer the campfire.

Campfire Dinner

Ingredients
1 pound(s)lean hamburger
6potatoes
3-4carrots
1 medium to large onion
4slice(s)bacon
seasoning
Directions
Make hamburger into 4 patties. Slice the potatoes, carrots, and onion. Place 1 hamburger pattie, 1/4 of the potatoes, carrots, and onions on a piece of aluminum foil, large enough to wrap around all ingredients. Add 1slice of bacon, halved. Season with your preferred seasonings. Wrap all ingredients in the foil, and seal well. I then wrap it again. Place in a bed of coals for approximately 15 minutes, turn and cook for another 15 minutes. Cooking time varies, so just keep checking. Variations can include mushrooms, peas, or anything else desired.

Campfire Eggs

Makes: 4
Ingredients
8 slice(s) bacon
1 1/2 c frozen hash browns
1/2 c onions
6 eggs
1/3 c milk
1/4 tsp salt
1/2 c shredded cheddar or colby cheese
Directions
Cook bacon in a heavy skillet until crisp. Remove and crumble bacon. Pour off all but 2 tablespoons of fat. Add onion to the pan with the potatoes, sprinkle with salt and pepper. Return to heat (fire) and fry until potatoes are lightly browned. Beat together eggs, milk, 1/4 tsp. salt and pepper to taste. Pour over browned potatoes in skillet. Cook without stirring until mixture begins to set. Using a spatula, lift and fold partially cooked eggs so uncooked egg flows underneath. Continue cooking for about 4 minutes until cooked but not dry. Arrange crumbled bacon on top, sprinkle with cheese. Breakfast in a skillet!

Campfire French Fries

Makes: 1

Ingredients

1 medium potato, cut into strips
seasoning salt and pepper to taste
1 Tbsp Parmesan cheese
1 Tbsp margarine
1 Tbsp bacon bits

Directions

Place potato on large square of heavy duty foil. Sprinkle with seasoning salt, pepper and cheese; toss to coat. Dot with margarine; sprinkle with bacon bits. Seal foil, leaving steam vent on top. Grill over hot coals for 30-45 min or until potatoes are tender, turning occasionally.

Campfire Fudge

Ingredients
1 cNestle Semi-Sweet chococlate chips
2/3csweetened condensed milk
1 Tbspwater
1/2cgranola cereal
Directions
In large saucepan, combine chocolate chips, sweetened condensed milk and water. Melt over low heat, stirring constantly, until chocolate chips melt and mixture is smooth. Remove from heat. Pour into foil-lined 8" square pan. Sprinkle top with granola cereal. Let stand until firm (about 1 hour). Cut into 1" squares.

Campfire Onion

Ingredients
1 large onion
1/4c butter
1 beef bouillon cube
1 Tbsp Worchester sauce
1 tsp fresh garlic
Directions
Hollow out the center of the large onion, add butter, bouillon, worchester and garlic. Cover completely with aluminum foil and place over the campfire on a rack for approximately 45 minutes.

Campfire Pineapple Upsidedown Cakes

Ingredients
1 box glazed doughnuts (6 - 8)
1 can pineapple rings
12 - 16pats of butter
6 - 8marachino cherries
6 - 8tspbrown sugar
Directions
Prepare 1 large square aluminum foil per each serving. Place 1 pat of butter in center of foil. Place 1 pineapple ring on top of butter and 1 doughnut on top of pineapple. Add 1 tsp. Brown Sugar into doughnut hole. Add another pat of butter on top of brown sugar. Top with 1 Marachino cherry. Bring sides of foil over top of dessert and twist top. Place on campfire grill near low heat & cook 5-10 minutes.

Campfire Potatoes And Onions

Ingredients
2-3pound(s)white or red potatoes
1 medium to large onion
6-8slice(s)bacon
1-2Tbspolive oil
Directions
Cut onion and potatoes into chunks. Lay out foil into a "pan". Lay 3 to 4 slices of bacon on the bottom, then add onions and potatoes. Add oil and top with remaining bacon. Wrap tightly. Grill 20 to 25 minutes and then flip foil packet over and cook an additional 2- minutes.

Campfire Potatoes

Ingredients
potatoes
butter
salt
Directions
Wash potatoes and add butter and salt, then wrap in aluminum foil and place on grill

Campfire Roasted Turkey

Ingredients
1 8-12 pound Turkey
salt and pepper
seasonings

Directions
Season the turkey with salt and pepper and a seasoning blend (if desired). Place a meat rack in the bottom of a 14" deep Dutch oven, spray with oil. If stuffing turkey, pack loosely. Place turkey on the rack. The sides of the turkey should not be touching the Dutch oven. Cover and start on low hook over medium fire. When the turkey begins to cook (steam and sizzle), raise to higher #2 hook and continue cooking. When meat thermometer reaches nearly done stage, remove from fire, add top coals to brown and finish cooking. Roasting time for 8 to 12 lb. turkey is 2-3/4 to 3 hours, if stuffed 3 to 3-1/2 hours. Turkey is done when internal temperature reaches 180°F, stuffing 165°F.

Campfire Stew With Hambuger

Ingredients
1 pound(s)ground beef
1/2large onion
1 large can of Campbell's Vegetable Soup
Directions
Brown ground beef and onion. Drain. Add vegetable soup and heat till hot. This can be made in a dutch oven over a fire, on the camper stove or in an electric skillet.

Campfire Stew

Ingredients
1 pound(s)ground beef
1 small onion, chopped
1 small can stewed tomatoes (optional)
1 can (10 3/4 oz.) Campbell's chicken gumbo soup
1 can Veg All
salt and pepper to taste
garlic powder to taste (optional)
Directions
Brown ground beef and onion, Drain Grease. Add rest of ingredients, stir and cover for 10 to 15 minutes. Serve with buttered bread.

Campfire Stir Fry

Ingredients
1 package Hilshire Farm Lite Polska Kielbasa
4beef tenderloin fillets
1 red pepper
1/2small onion
1/4colive oil
1/2cbutter
salt and pepper to taste
Directions
Slice the Polska Kielbasa and meat into bite size pieces. Slice the pepper and onion. Put into a disposable aluminum 13x9 inch pan and cook over the fire until meat is cooked to your liking!
Great served with potatoes and mushrooms:
1/2 stick butter
1tbs olive oil
1 15oz can sliced white pototoes
1 8oz or 4oz can sliced mushrooms
Cook over fire in round or square aluminum cake pan. Cook only until heated through.

Campfire Sweet Potatoes

Ingredients
1 large can of sweet potato's drained
1/2c apple butter
1 Tbsp honey
1 Tbsp brown sugar
1 tsp lemon juice
half a stick of butter
1/2tsp cinnamon or nutmeg
Directions
Cut a big piece of foil to make a packet. Drain sweet potatoes and mix apple butter, honey, brown sugar, lemon juice. Pour over potatoes, cut up butter and dot potatoes. Sprinkel cinnamon or nutmeg over potatoes. Wrap in foil, grill in oven or on grill for 10 minutes, carefully remove and ENJOY!!!!!

Campfire Tacos

Ingredients
4medium potatos
2pound(s)precooked ground beef
1 package shredded cheese
1 package taco seasoning
1 can black olives
1 package sour cream
Directions
Cube potatoes and put in a foil packet put in fire for 1/2 hour. While cooking potatoes, place thawed meat in a pan on camp stove and add 1 cup water and taco seasoning. When potatoes and meat are done. Place potatoes in a bowl and add meat, top with cheese and all other taco items.

Campground Chicken Salad

Ingredients
1 5 oz. can Swanson Boned chicken or turkey, cut up
2 hard-cooked eggs, chopped
1/4c chopped sweet pickle
2 Tbsp minced onion
1 tsp mustard
salt
pepper
Directions
Lightly mix chicken, eggs, pickle, onion and mustard; season to taste with salt and pepper. Serve as a sandwich filling or on crackers.

Camping Margarita's

Ingredients
1/2can frozen limeaid (Minute Maid is best)
1/4cTriple Sec
1/2cgold tequila
Directions
Put ingredients in blender, fill rest of blender with ice. Blend on high till smooth. Rim glasses with salt by dipping glass in mixture then in margarita salt. Preferably glasses that have battery lights in stems and can light up. Pour and enjoy.

Camping Potatoes

Ingredients
4 large potatoes
2 celery stalks
4 cubes butter
1 medium onion
parsley
salt and pepper
water

Directions
Cut aluminum foil into 4, 12X12 inch squares. Dice potatoes, onions and celery into 1 inch cubes or smaller. (1" for potatoes, smaller for celery and onions). Put all diced items into a bowl, add salt, pepper, and parsley to your liking. Mix up until all ingredients are thouroughly combined. Place equal amounts from the bowl onto seperate pieces of the aluminum foil squares you cut. Add butter to your liking to each group. Wrap up foil around your mixture leaving a small opening. Pour about a 1/4 cup of water into each and crimp the hole shut. Place on grill or over the fire for about 20 minutes or until potatoes are soft. Empty into a bowl and enjoy.

Camping Rice Pudding

Makes: 4

Ingredients
1 cinstant rice
1/2cdry milk
1/4craisins
2 Tbspsugar
1/4tspcinnamon
1 1/2cwater
Directions
Put the ingredients into a zippered baggie and mix. Bring 1 1/2 cup water to a rolling boil. Add contents of baggie and stir thoroughly. Remove from heat, cover, and let sit, stirring occasionally for 7minutes. Serve warm or cooled.

Camping Spaghetti

Ingredients
1 pound(s)hamburger
onion
salt and pepper
2 large cans of Franco American spaghetti
Directions
Brown hamburger, flavoring with some onion, salt & pepper, etc. Drain, add a couple lg. cans of Franco American spaghetti. Serve with a salad or bread and butter. Cooking it like this totally changes the flavor of the canned spaghetti. I like to think of it as a camper's hamburger helper. We love it! It can be cooked on the grill or stove.

Camping Stew

Ingredients
1 package hot dogs, sliced or 1 pound browned hamburger
sauteed onions (optional)
1 can Bean and Bacon soup
1 can corn
1 can lima beans
1 can potatoes (diced small)
1 can green beans
other canned vegetables of choice
Directions
Bring this to a boil over campfire or other heat source and simmer. Season to taste. Stew is even better when made a day ahead and let the flavors meld. Enjoy!

Camp-Out Tomatoes

Ingredients
4 -5large tomatoes
medium sized red onion
bottle red-raspberry viniagrette dressing
Directions
Cut tomatoes and onion into bite-sized pieces. Place in zip-lock bag and pour in entire bottle of dressing. Allow to marinate overnight in cooler. Pour contents of bag into pot on camping stove or over fire and allow to boil/simmer for 30 minutes.

Cheddar Spam & Potatoes

Ingredients
1 can Spam, diced
4medium potatoes, diced
1 small onion, diced
8 oz. package shredded cheddar cheese
1/2stick margarine
Directions
Place in hot bag or foil diced spam, potatoes and onion and margarine. Place on grill of hot coals or very small fire. Let cook until potatoes are done, approximately 1/2 hour to 45 minutes turning over occasionally not to burn. When done, open bag or foil and sprinkle with shredded cheese.

Cheese On The Cob

Ingredients
1/2c mayonnaise
5 ears of corn, husked and cleaned
1 c fresh shredded Parmesan cheese
chili powder
salt
black pepper
Directions
Prepare grill. Brush a thin layer of mayonnaise on corn. Sprinkle the corn with cheese, light amount of chili powder, salt and pepper. Wrap each ear of corn in foil, and place each on the grill. Turn occasionally and cook for 10 minutes or until kernels begin to brown. Serve warm......Enjoy.

Cheesy Veggie Chowder

Makes: 8
Ingredients
4c chicken broth
8 stalks celery (sliced)
4 carrots (sliced)
2 medium potatoes (peeled and cubed)
1 large onion (chopped)
1 tsp black pepper
2 c whote kernel corn (frozen)
1/4c butter
3/4c all-purpose flour
2 c milk
2 c cheddar cheese (shredded)
Directions
Add vegetables to chicken broth and bring to a low boil for about 20 minutes. While vegetables are cooking, melt butter in a skillet. Slowly add flour, stirring constantly. Add milk and stir until thoroughly mixed. Stir in cheese until completely melted. Add cheese sauce to vegetables. Stir. Cook at a medium low heat until vegetables are of desired tenderness.

Cherry Dessert

Ingredients
1 can crushed pineapple
1 can cherry pie filling
1 box white cake mix (dry)
1 stick melted margarine
1 c chopped pecans
Directions
Oil Dutch Oven. Layer in the order given. Bake at 350 degrees for 45-50 minutes.

In order to control the temperature of your Dutch Oven: add 3 to the circumference of the lid, and subtract 3 for the bottom number. This will give you the number of hot coals of charcoal that you need to achieve 350 degrees. (example) A 10" Dutch Oven would need 13 coals on top and 7 underneath.

Chicken Asparagus

Ingredients
4 chicken breasts
1 can Cream of Mushroom Soup
1 can Aspargus Spears
2 tsp salt
1/2 tsp pepper
1/2-1 tsp garlic salt
4 slice(s) provolone cheese

Directions
Tear off four squares of aluminum foil approximately 6 inches long. Wash chicken and remove skin if desired. Spray each sheet of foil with Pam oil. Place chicken breast in center of sprayed foil (bone side down) and sprinkle salt, pepper, and garlic salt on. Place one slice of cheese on top of spices, (one slice per breast), and then add the asparagus. Wrap sides and ends together and bake in the oven at 300 degrees for approximately 90 minutes or on the grill until the chicken is done. This is very low in carbohydrates.

Chicken Cacciatore

Ingredients
1 frying chicken
1 bell pepper
1 white onion
8ozsliced mushrooms
3 cloves of garlic
1/4colive oil
1 large jar of spaghetti sauce
1 Tbspdry oregano
1/4cfresh basil
1/2cred wine
salt and pepper
Directions
Cut up chicken into pieces, chop bell pepper, onion, garlic, and fresh basil. Heat olive oil in Dutch Oven or over coals until hot. Brown onions and garlic, add chicken pieces (turning to brown on both sides) and red wine. Stir in bell pepper, mushrooms, spaghetti sauce and salt & pepper and herbs. Cover with lid and add coals to the top. Cook 30 to 45 minutes. Serve with/over white rice or pasta. I like to prep all my ingredients into plastic bags at home. You can also add zucchini, eggplant, fresh tomatoes, squash, Italian sausage or anything you like.

Chicken In A Bag

Ingredients
1 pound(s)chicken breast
2 crice
1/2pound(s)frozen peas
1/2pound(s)shredded cheddar cheese
Directions
You will need one small roll of aluminum foil (heavy gauge is better) and 4 sticks (about 1/2-1 inch in diameter). At home, cut chicken breast into cubes and fully cook in a skillet. Season with lemon pepper if you like. Cook rice, remove from pot and let cool. In a large container, combine chicken, rice, frozen peas, and shredded cheddar cheese. Cover and refrigerate. At dinner time, scoop each serving onto the middle of a 2 ft. long piece of aluminum foil. (four servings = four pieces of aluminum foil). Wrap the mixture into the foil by folding the foil longwise (so that it stays about 2 ft. long). Wrap the tail ends of the aluminum around a heavy stick and warm each wrapped mixture over a campfire until the cheese melts. The foil cools rapidly and can be unwrapped easily from around the sticks and from around the mixture. You could also add cashews, canned mushrooms, and/or soy sauce depending on the tastes of the group.

Chicken Pie

Ingredients
2 Pillsbury pie crusts
2 chicken breasts, boiled
1 can peas and carrots or mixed vegetables (drained)
1 can cream of chicken soup
1/4c milk
Directions
Bake at 400 degrees for 30 to 35 minutes or until crust is browned. Makes 1 9" pie.

Chicken Salsa Stir-Fry

Ingredients
1 pound(s) skinless chicken breast tenders
2 Tbsp olive oil
1 c thick and chunky mild salsa
1 frozen stir fry vegetables (12-16 oz. package)
1/2 tsp garlic powder (optional)
1/2 c mozarella cheese

Directions
Mix vegetables, olive oil, and salsa in a bowl. Place in a piece of heavy duty foil (18 inches in length), sprayed with non-stick cooking spray. Place chicken tenders, singly, on top of vegetable mix and sprinkle with garlic powder. Seal foil to form a long rectangular shape. Place over an open fire and cook approximately 20-30 minutes depending on how hot your fire is. Check every 10 minutes or so. When chicken juices run clear, sprinkle cheese over the chicken and loosely seal foil until cheese is melted. Feeds 4. You could also serve this with rice.

Chip-A-S'mores

Makes: 1
Ingredients
2chocolate chip cookies
1 marshmallow
1 square piece of a chocolate bar
Directions
Toast a marshmallow over your campfire, take your cookies and put the chocolate and marshmallow in it like a sandwich and eat up, when done, repeat!

Chocolate-Peanut Butter Wraps

Ingredients
1/2c creamy peanut butter
4 8-inch flour tortillas
1 c miniature marshmallows
1/2c miniature semisweet chocolate chips
Directions
Spread 2 tablespoons of peanut butter on each tortilla. Sprinkle 1/4 cup of marshmallows and 2 tablespoons of chocolate chips on half of each tortilla. Roll up, beginning with the topping side. Wrap each tortilla in heavy-duty foil; seal tightly. Grill, covered, over low heat for 5 to 10 minutes or until heated through. Unwrap and eat.

Chuck Wagon

Ingredients
1 pound(s)ground beef (extra lean)
1 can whole kernel corn
1 can diced tomatoes
1 cmacaroni wagon wheels (or elbow macaroni)
salt and pepper
Directions
Put macaroni in one quart of cold water and bring to a boil. Remove from heat. Brown ground beef, then drain any pools of grease. Drain macaroni, then add the browned beef to it. Drain water from can of whole kernel corn and in with the macaroni and beef. Dump the whole can of tomatoes (with the liquid) into the mixture and bring to a boil. Remove from heat. Serve and season to taste.

Chunky Chill Chaser

Ingredients
1 can (19 oz.) Campbell's Chunky Beef Soup
2 tsp catsup
1 tsp mustard
dash hot pepper sauce
Directions
In saucepan, combine all ingredients. Heat; stirring occasionally.

Citrus Trout

Ingredients
3 -4pound(s)lake trout
1 orange
1 lemon
1 lime
salt & pepper
butter & oil

Directions
Gut fish and remove head. Thinly slice the lemon, orange and lime. Lightly rub the cavity of the fish with salt. Place fruit slices in cavity with a couple of dabs of butter. Lightly oil the outside of the fish and wrap in tin foil making sure of a good seal. Cook on each side for about 10 mins. Fish will flake off the bones.

Clam Chowder

Ingredients
4 oz salt pork (diced)
1 onion (finely chopped)
1/4 c diced celery
3 potatoes (diced)
1 c clam juice
1 c water
1/4 tsp ground thyme
2 c milk
2 c light cream
4 dozen large clams

Directions

Brown salt pork and remove from Dutch oven. In rendered fat, sauté onions and celery until tender. Add potatoes, clam juice, water, thyme, and salt and pepper to taste. Simmer uncovered until potatoes are tender. Stir in milk, cream, and clams. Heat through, but do not boil.

Coconut Lime Layer Cake

Ingredients
2 large limes (juice and zest)
1 c sweetened shredded coconut
1 1/4 c self-rising flour
3/4 c sugar
1 1/2 sticks butter (room temperature)
3 large eggs (lightly beaten)
1 1/2 tsp baking powder

Directions
Pour coconut into a small bowl and add lime juice. Let the coconut absorb the lime juice for one hour. In large bowl, sift the flour. Mix in all other cake ingredients, including the lime zest and coconut. Beat until thoroughly combined. Use two Dutch ovens to make two 8" cake layers. Bake for 20 minutes.

Coffee Can Chicken

Ingredients
1 whole chicken (no more than 3 1/2 lbs)
butter
salt
pepper
heavy duty aluminum foil
Directions
Punch or drill holes in gallon size tin can 1 inch up from the bottom and spaced 1 inch apart around the can. Place 18 briquettes (no more no less) in the bottom of the can and light. (The can gets hot enough to burn the grass below it so be very careful where you place the can.) Rub chicken with butter and season as you like. Wrap chicken with heavy aluminum foil twice. (First in the side to side direction and then from bottom to top. Make sure foil closing point is on the top of the chicken.) Once charcoal has turned white, place the chicken into the can with the legs facing the top of the can. It's perfectly fine if the chicken sticks out of the can. Leave the can and chicken sit for 3 hours. When 3 hours has past you can remove the chicken from the can and when you open the foil the chicken will be fall off the bone tender, juicy and delicious.

Corn On The Cob With Bacon

Ingredients
husked corn on the cob
raw bacon slices
parmesan cheese
Directions
Wrap a whole slice of bacon around each ear of corn after generously sprinkling on the parmesan cheese. Then wrap each cob securely in aluminum foil, twisting the ends. Cook on the rack over the campfire or on the grill, turning often, for about 35 minutes. No need for butter or salt due to the bacon.

Corn On The Cob

Ingredients
4ears of corn
butter or margarine
salt and pepper
Directions
Remove husks from corn. Spread corn generously with butter or margarine and sprinkle with salt and pepper. Wrap each ear in foil, sealing and twisting foil around ends. Place on grill over hot coals for 15 to 20 minutes or till tender, turning often.

Corn Roasted In Foil On Coals

Ingredients
corn on the cob
butter or margarine
Directions
With husks: Remove outer husks on cob corn. Peel back the inner husks, but do not remove. Clean any silk and remove. Spread soft butter or margarine over the corn. Pull the husk back over the corn. Wrap in heavy -duty aluminum foil. Lay on the as gray coals for 20 to 30 minutes, turning once.
Without husks: Remove husks and silk. Place on piece of heavy-duty aluminum foil. Add 1 tablespoon of butter or margarine and 2 tablespoons of water. Wrap securely and lay on the coals or grill. Takes about 20 to 30 minutes to heat through.

Corn Roasted On Girl Over Coals

Ingredients
corn on the cob with husks
butter or margarine
salt and pepper to taste
Directions
Remove the large outer husks of cob corn. Turn back the inner husks, but do not completely remove. Clean any silk and remove. Spread the corn with butter or margarine. Pull the husks back over the corn and tie with fine wire. Place over the hot coals or grill and turn frequently until heated through, about 20 to 30 minutes. Serve with salt and pepper and MORE BUTTER!

Cornish Game Hen

Ingredients
cornish game hens
bacon
Directions
Wrap the hen in your favorite bacon and wrap in foil. Cook over fire and place in hot but indirect heat for about 25-35 minutes or longer-depending on how hot the flames are. The hen will have a nice smoky flavor from the bacon and remain very moist. Goes with anything.

Cowboy Stew

Ingredients
1 15 oz. can chili with beans
1 pound(s)lean ground beef
1 14 oz. can barbecue baked beans
1 onion, chopped
1/4cshredded cheese
Directions
Brown the beef and onion and drain the grease. Pour the chili and beans and simmer for 30 minutes. Top with cheese and enjoy!
I brown the beef and onion ahead of time. Freeze. Then pack it in the cooler.

Cowboy Turn Spit Game Hens

Makes: 12
Ingredients
12Cornish game hens
1 bottle Jack Daniel's Horseradish mustard
1 bottle Jack Daniel's Old No. 7 BBQ sauce
1 cwater
6TbspCampfire Cafe Garlic Butter TM spice
Directions
Season the hens with Garlic ButterTM spice and line them up on the Turn Spit. We made as many as we could fit on the Spit; you make what you need for your crew. Hang the spit up about 3/4 of the distance between the crossbar and the fire, over a medium fire with a good bed of coals. Give it 1/4 turn about every 20 minutes, for about 1-1/2 hours. Hens are done when juices run clear. Thin the mustard with a little water in a small bowl. Once hens begin to cook, baste with the mustard and BBQ

sauce. Cook until done. Split down the middle, place on platter, and serve with Chicken & Dumplings.

Cream Cheese Chicken

Ingredients
1 package Good Season Italian Dressing mix
3-4 chicken breasts, raw, cubed
1/2 c butter
1 can Cream of Chicken soup
3/4 c cream cheese
Directions
Combine dressing, chicken and butter in crockpot. Cook for 4 hours on high, 6 hours on low. Take chicken out and add remaining ingredients, mixing well. Return chicken to crockpot and cook on high for ½ hour. Serve with noodles.

Crockpot Vegetable Beef Soup

Ingredients
1 pound(s) stew meat
1 can tomatoes
baby carrots
1 small onion
2 medium potatoes, cubed
1 stalk celery, chopped
1 package frozen, mixed vegetables
1 beef boullion cube
water
Directions
Place all ingredients in crock pot, add water to barely cover. Stir thoroughly. Cover crockpot, and cook 10 - 12 hours

Cruncchy Oriental Coleslaw Salad

Ingredients
1/3clight olive oil
1 package (3 ounces) chicken flavored Ramen Noodles
1/2tspgarlic powder
1 package (16 ounces) shredded coleslaw mix
1 package (5 ounces) sliced almonds

Directions
Put coleslaw mix and almonds in a bowl, sprinkle garlic powder and seasoning packet from noodles over slaw mix. Heat oil in microwave for 1minute and pour over slaw and mix. Crush the noodles and mix in slaw. You can add sunflower seeds or any type of nuts that you like. This is a fast and easy side dish for burgers or hotdogs, or any type of sandwich when you are camping. You can mix everything but the noodles ahead of time add the noodles right before serving.

Darrell's Mexican Casserole

Ingredients
2pound(s)hamburger or ground turkey
2taco seasoning packets
2cans rotel tomatoes
2packages shreaded cheese (cheddar and Mexican mixed)
2cans ranch style beans
2cans cream of mushroom soup
1 small can sliced black olives
2 green onions (diced)
1 pickled jalapeno (sliced)
1 package tortillas (20)
Directions

Brown hamburger meat and drain, mix everything but cheese, sliced jalapeno and tortillas (hold back some black olives for the top), heat and bring to boil, cut tortillas as needed into strips, oil and preheat dutch oven, layer with mixture, cheese and then tortillas, ending with cheese (for example, do mixture, cheese, tortillas, mixture, etc.), cover and bake at 375 for 30-45 minutes then uncover for 15 minutes and remove from oven and let stand for 5 minutes. Cut into squares.

Day Camp Stew

Ingredients
1 1/2pound(s)ground beef
1 medium yellow onion
2 cans kidney beans
2-3cans stewed tomatoes
2 cans sliced baby potatoes
2 bay leaves
garlic to taste
worcestershire sauce
salt and pepper to taste
Directions
You can have 2 - 3 cans of stewed tomatoes, depending on how much soup you want. In a pot, brown the meat and onion together. Add the bay leaves and worcestershire sauce, then cook until meat is done and onions are translucent. Drain the beans and add to the pot. Add the stewed tomatoes. Drain the potatoes and add them to the pot. Add Salt and pepper to taste. Simmer until all the ingredients are hot. Ladle into bowls and serve with French bread.

Delicious Poached Salmon

Ingredients
half of salmon filleted (or large piece of salmon)
1 cchopped onion
dill, fresh or in spice jar
1 12 oz. can beer
butter
Directions
Use 2 disposable aluminum pans and place 1 cup of water in bottom pan. Place salmon skin side down and sprinkle with dill. Dot with butter and cover with onions and beer. Set double pans with salmon on grate over an open fire for 35 minutes. Keep the fire going with a low flame.

Deluxe Steamed Green Beans

Ingredients
fresh green beans
2Tbspbutter
2 - 3cloves garlic, minced
8oz. fresh mushrooms, rinsed and quartered
salt and pepper
Directions
Construct a dish out of heavy duty tin foil. Rinse and snap the ends off of one pound (more or less) of fresh green beans and heap on the tinfoil dish. Add fresh garlic, quartered mushrooms, butter (in chunks) and salt and pepper to taste. Seal up the whole dish tightly, using an extra piece of tin foil wrapped around the whole thing. (From experience, it is best to keep all seals facing up) Place on your campfire grill over indirect heat, I.e. not over an open flame. Once you hear them steaming, allow to cook for 10 to 15 minutes. Open carefully, serve and enjoy! Can also add onion, zucchini, or squash if desired.

Deviled Eggs

Ingredients
2 dozen large eggs (hard-boiled)
1 c mayonnaise
1/2 c dill pickle relish
1/4 c green onions
dash cayenne pepper
1 can sliced black olives
1 can sliced green olives
Directions
Slice boiled eggs in half and remove yolks. Combine yolks with mayo, pickle relish, green onions and blend until creamy. Fill egg whites with yolk mixture using cake decorator - or with a small spoon - and sprinkle with cayenne pepper. Garnish with olive slices. Makes 24

Dilled Peas & Potatoes

Ingredients
8 small new red potatoes (1-1/2 pounds)
1 pound(s) sugar snap peas (fresh or frozen)
1/2 c olive oil
6 Tbsp white wine vinegar
2 Tbsp fresh dill, minced
1/2 tsp salt
1/2 tsp freshly ground pepper
6 green onions (chopped)
Directions
Cook potatoes in Dutch oven in boiling water until tender; drain and thinly slice. Cook snap peas until crisp-tender; drain and plunge in cold water to stop cooking; drain again. Whisk together oil and next 4 ingredients. Add to sliced potatoes, snap

peas, and onions, tossing gently to coat. Cover and chill 2 hours, or serve warm.

Doctored Up Pork & Beans

Ingredients
1 16 oz. can pork and beans
1/2 onion, chopped
2 tsp brown sugar, packed
1/4 tsp dry mustard
1/4 c ketchup
2 slices of bacon, chunked and fried until crispy
Directions
Combine all ingredients and simmer for 30 minutes. More bacon may be used if desired.

Dog Gone Good Doggies

Ingredients
Hot Dogs
Bacon
Onion
BBQ Sauce
Pickle Spears
Foil
Buns (optional)
Directions
Wrap a hot dog with a slice of bacon. Put it on a double layer of foil, add chopped onion, bbq sauce and a pickle spear, wrap foil around it and place it right in the campfire coals for 10 minutes. Unwrap and enjoy with a bun or without.

Donuts Surprise!

Ingredients
cake doughnuts, cut in half like a bagel
favorite fruit, sliced apples, pineapple rings, peaches, berries etc.
1/2csugar
3 Tbspcinnamon
Directions
Cut cake doughnuts in half like a bagel and add the fruit of your choice- fresh sliced apples, canned or fresh rings pineapples, canned or fresh peaches etc. Add 1/2 cup sugar and 3tablespoons. of cinnamon - adjust to your taste. Replace the top half of the doughnut, wrap in foil and place in embers or over the grill for 5 - 7 minutes. Use different fruits and it will be a great breakfast surprise to see who gets what kind.

Dutch Oven Chicken

Ingredients
4-6boneless chicken breasts
4-6large pieces of country ham
2cans of mushroom soup
Directions
Start a fire. Place chicken in the Dutch oven. Place the country ham slices on top of the chicken. Pour the mushroom soup over chicken and ham. Put the lid on. Place oven in the fire and put some hot briquettes on the lid of the dutch oven. This takes about 1 hour to cook.

Dutch Oven Cobbler

Ingredients
2cans crushed pineapple

3cans cherry pie filling
1 package yellow cake mix
1/2cbutter
1 cwalnuts or pecans
Directions
Start with a hot fire and bed of coals. Grease the dutch oven thoroughly. Add ingredients to dutch oven in the above order and spread evenly, but DO NOT MIX TOGETHER. Top with pats of butter and sprinkle with nuts if desired. Close lid and seal. Place dutch oven on bed of 15-25 coals, evenly spaced for even cooking. Place 10-15 coals on top of lid to heat from the top. Allow approximately 30 minutes for cooking. Check the cobbler by carefully lifting the lid (do not drop in coals or ashes), then put a knife in it and if it comes out clean, it is ready. The pie filling should be bubbling up around the edges and through the crust. Let it cool and enjoy alone or with whipped cream or vanilla ice cream.

Dutch Oven Stuffed Peppers

Ingredients
4large green bell peppers
1 1/2pound(s)hamburger
1 can Vegetable Beef soup
1 package Lipton Beefy Onion dry soup mix
1 egg
Directions
Cut the top off the green pepper and clean out. Retain the tops. Mix together all the ingredients, then form into 4 balls. Fill each green pepper with a hamburger ball and then replace the top of the pepper. Place the peppers on a wire rack in the bottom of the Dutch oven. Cover with the lid. Place 12 hot Briquettes under the Dutch oven, 10-12 an inch apart around the lid of the Dutch oven, and two on each side of the handle in the middle.

Cook for 1 1/2-2 hours. Every 30 minutes add fresh hot coals to the bottom and top of the oven and rotate the oven one quarter of a turn. The tops of the peppers may turn dark brown, but cook until the meat reaches the doneness level you prefer.

Easy Barbecue Sauce

Ingredients
2medium onions, sliced
3/4cketchup
3/4cwater
2TbspWorcestershire sauce
2Tbspvinegar (white or apple cider)
1 tspchili powder
1 tspgarlic powder
salt and pepper to taste
Directions
Combine all in saucepan and simmer for 45 minutes.

Easy Campfire Corn

Ingredients
ear of corn
butter
salt
Directions
Shuck the ear of corn, rub with butter and sprinkle with salt. Wrap corn in foil, cook in campfire or coals for about 15 minutes. Be extremely careful when unwrapping the foil and corn will be hot.

Easy Campfire Mushrooms

Ingredients
whole mushrooms
Worcestershire sauce
A - 1 Sauce
butter (optional)
Directions
Wash mushrooms. Place mushrooms in center of aluminum foil and generously sprinke Worcestershire sauce on top. I add a minimal amount of A-1 as well. You can add a tablespoon or two of butter, if you want. Fold aluminum foil making sure everything is sealed and barbeque until mushrooms are juicy and cooked through. The mushrooms produce their own juice, but be careful not to overcook, as they can dry out if cooked too long!

Easy Campfire Peach Cobbler

Ingredients
2packages yellow cake mix
4cans sliced peaches
1 stick butter
Directions
Pour peaches in bottom of 14" Dutch oven. Sprinkle cake mix over top of fruit. Do not stir. Cut pats of butter and place evenly on surface. Cover and bake over medium heat until bubbly and top is lightly browned, approximately 30-45 minutes. Kitchen Directions: Bake at 350° for 40 minutes.

Easy Campfire Pizza

Ingredients

flour tortillas
pizza sauce
shredded mozzerella cheese
pizza toppings: pepperoni, olives, mushrooms, pineapple etc.
Directions
Cover one side of a flour tortilla with pizza sauce, cheese and topping. Fold tortilla in half or place another tortilla on top. Wrap gently with foil and place in wire handheld campfire basket or on grate over hot coals until cheese is melted. It doesn't take long and you've got a meal kids and adults alike will love.

Easy Campfire Stew

Ingredients
2pound(s)ground beef
2large cans of campbells ABC vegetable soup
salt and pepper to taste
Directions
Brown ground beef in large skillet; drain; add two large cans of soup. Simmer and Enjoy! MMM MMMM GOOOD!!! Happy Camping!

Easy Home Pries

Ingredients
sliced canned potatoes
onion flakes
bread crumbs
Italian seasoning
Directions

Add onion flakes to sliced canned potatoes. Sprinkle with bread crumbs mixed with Italian seasoning. Fry on grill for 10-15 min and you have easy home fries.

Easy Pigs'n A Blanket

Ingredients
sliced bread
butter
cheese slices
hot dogs
Directions
Take 2 slices of bread, butter one side of each piece. Cook over fire till golden brown on the buttered side. Put a cheese slice on unbuttered side of one piece of bread, melt cheese. Put a hot dog diagonally on top of the cheese so ends of hot dog are at corners of bread. Roll hot dog up in the sandwich & fold over to make a wrap. Repeat to make more.

Easy Rice Recipe

Ingredients
1 box "quick" white rice
2 cans chicken broth
fresh green beans or favorite green vegetable
Directions
Make an easy packet with foil and add rice, chicken broth, and place green vegetable of your choice right on top. Fold up foil packet tightly and place on BBQ for 20 minutes.

Esay Taco Salad

Makes: 4
Ingredients
1 1/2pound(s)hamburger
shredded lettuce
2cgrated cheddar cheese
2chopped tomatoes
1 csalsa
1 csour cream
1 bag tortilla chips
1 package taco seasoning mix
Directions
Cook hamburger on the stove or in a frying pan over the fire. Follow the directions on the taco seasoning package. Place all the ingredients on the table with serving spoons and then everyone can make their own taco salad, starting with the chips and layering ingredients of their choice.

Easy Taco Soup

Ingredients
2cans stewed tomatoes
1/2pound(s)ground beef`
1 can Rotel tomatoes
1 onion
2 cans jalepeno pinto beans
1 package taco seasoning mix
2 cans corn
1 package ranch dressing mix
Directions
Chop up the onion. Brown beef with onion; drain. Add remaining ingredients, including all the liquid. Bring to a boil and simmer for 30 minutes.

Easy Tostadas

Ingredients
1 can chili
1 small bag Fritos
cheese
lettuce
salsa
tomatoes
sour cream
green onions
olives
Directions
Heat chili in can over fire (after opening) and layer a plate with the rest of the ingredients.

Eggs In A Bag

Ingredients
2eggs per person
1 freezer ziploc quart bag
cheese
bacon
tomatoes
Directions
Boil large pot of water. Crack 2 eggs into ziploc bag. Add your ingredients. Close bag, but leave some air in the bag. Mush up your eggs until mixed well. Put bag into boiling water. Boil for 10-12 minutes. Open bag, and release on to plate. Enjoy!
If you are serving more than one person, use a Sharpie Permanent Marker and add each persons name to there respective bags.

Fire Pit Potatoes

Ingredients
russet potatoes (1 per person)
onions
butter
garlic salt
pepper
heavy duty foil
Directions
Thinly slice potatoes and layer them in the foil spreading them out as you go down in a row. Put pats of butter on the top then sprinkle them with garlic salt and pepper. Thinly slice onions on top. Fold together and make little pouches. Put on the fire and let them cook approx.15 min. Cook longer if you like them crispy. They are super easy and very good.

Fireside Fajita's

Ingredients
1-2pound(s)round steak or chicken tenders
1 12 ounce jar of salsa
1 package fajita seasoning
1 can Mexicorn or yellow corn
1 bag frozen stir fry onions/peppers
1 Tbspflour
corn tortillas
Directions
I fix bags ahead of time in a Hot Bag (aluminum foil cooking bag or make your own). Slice steak or chicken into thin strips, then put all ingredients in a bag or foil, seal edges and place on rack over campfire coals. Let cook inside the bag for 20 to 30

minutes. Serve rolled up in warm soft corn tortilla or serve buffet style and add condiments of jalapeno's, Mexican blend cheeses, sour cream and Spanish rice and make your own.

Fish In Foil

Ingredients
fresh caught fish
salt
pepper
butter
lemon
Directions
Scale, gut, and clean fish. Salt, pepper, and add butter to fish on aluminum foil. Place one small lemon slice and butter in stomach cavity. Place on BBQ grill until cooked.

Fish Packets For Four

Ingredients
4fish fillets (salmon or trout)
2cuncooked minute rice
1 14 oz. can of chicken broth
1 cmatchstick carrots
1 tspMrs. Dash garlic and herb seasoning
1/3cfresh or dried chives
1 lemon
Directions
You will need heavy duty aluminum foil (4 pieces about 20 inches long) and butter or cooking spray to put on the aluminum foil pieces. Mix the rice and chicken broth in a bowl and let sit for a 5 minutes. Stir in carrots and seasoning. Slice your lemon. Place 1 fish per aluminum foil piece, put a little butter on the

inside of fish or on top, sprinkle a little Mrs. Dash seasoning on it and place a couple slices of lemon inside or on top of fish. Spoon rice mixture around fish, sprinkle fish with chives. Fold aluminum over fish so edges meet and seal edges making a tight 1/2 inch fold. Allow some space on sides for expansion and circulation. Grill packets about 5 inches from heat for 14 minutes or until fish flakes easily with fork. Fold back foil carefully, it's hot. Enjoy!

Foil Bag Surprise

Ingredients
1 package polish sausage, sliced
1 green pepper, sliced
1 onion, sliced
1 package fresh mushrooms, sliced
1 package hash browns or potatoes O'Brien
garlic powder
salt and pepper
Directions
Mix all of the ingredients in a foil bag. Roll up end to seal. When heated all the way through, cut a slit in the foil and serve out of the bag. NO DISHES TO CLEAN!!

Foil Dinner For One

Ingredients
1 potato
1/4 onion
1/4 bell pepper
1/2c baby carrots
1/4c sliced celery
canola oil spray

2 thin hamburger patties
seasoning salt
pepper or Mrs. Dash
1 Tbsp butter

Directions

Wash and scrub the potato, then slice. Slice the onion, pepper, and celery. Spread heavy duty aluminum foil out. Spray the foil with oil. Place one hamburger patty on foil. Lightly season with salt and pepper or Mrs. Dash. Layer vegetables over patty and lightly season. Lastly, place seasoned patty of hamburger on top. Add butter. Lay second sheet of aluminum foil over food. Carefully seal all edges of foil. Foil pockets can be substituted for sheets of foil. Non-stick foil may also be used. Cook over coals for 30 min., turning If using tongs, be careful to not puncture foil. Each person can individualize their meal with vegetables of choice. When your meal is cooked you can eat it right out of the foil. Length of cooking may be adjusted for larger or smaller quanities of food. If one patty is preferred, then you can divide meat in half and place it on top and bottom.

Foolproof Roast Chicken

Ingredients
4 chicken quarters or chicken pieces of your choice (skin on)
2 tsp salt
1/2 tsp pepper
bay leaves
1/3 olive oil
2 tsp minced garlic
1 Tbsp minced onion
1 tsp salt
1/4 tsp pepper
1/2 tsp powdered garlic
1/2 tsp Italian herbs

1/2tspparsley flakes (or 1 tsp fresh parsley, finely chopped)
1/4tspsage
1/4tspturmeric
dashpaprika

Directions

Boil your chicken pieces in a pot of water with salt, pepper, and a few bay leaves for 25-30 minutes - until meat is cooked through but not falling off the bone. Drain and let dry for a few minutes. The rest of the ingredients are for the sause. Mix together the sauce ingredients while chicken is cooking. "Paint" the sauce onto the cooked chicken with a pastry brush. Roast the chicken over a campfire or charcoal until the outside is golden brown or as done as you like. If you're stuck indoors, you can also broil or bake at 400+ degrees until desired doneness. Skin should be crispy when done.

Fresh Fruit Cake

Ingredients
1 capples (chopped)
1 cpears (chopped)
1 cpeaches (chopped)
2 csugar
1 cpecans (chopped)
3 cself-rising flour
1 tspcinnamon
1 tspnutmeg
1 cvegetable oil
1 tspvanilla
2 eggs
1/2cbrown sugar
1 stick butter

Directions

Line a 10" or a 12" Dutch oven with quick-release foil for this recipe. It is very dense and lining with foil will make it easier to remove the cake from the oven. Peel the peaches, and chop in small pieces. Chop apples and pears, but do not peel. Combine sugar, flour, and 1/2 cup of chopped pecans, cinnamon, nutmeg, oil, vanilla and eggs in large bowl. Mix all ingredients, then add the fruit and mix well. Pour batter into the lined Dutch oven. For topping, combine butter, remaining 1/2 cup pecans and brown sugar. Mix until blended, but crumbly, and spoon over top of cake batter. Bake for 20 minutes over a low fire on middle hook. Move to 2nd shortest hook, add top coals for 15 minutes; then remove from fire and continue baking for another 20 to 25 minutes. Toothpick will not come out clean, as this is a very dense, moist cake. Total baking time is about 1 hour 15 minutes. Kitchen directions: Bake 1 hr. 15 min. at 350°.

Frogmore Stew

Ingredients
16cwater
1/4cOld Bay seasoning
2lemons
2onions
4pound(s)small red potatoes
2pound(s)spicy smoked link sausage
6ears fresh corn
4pound(s)large shrimp (unpeeled)
garlic (optional)
seasoning salt
seafood cocktail sauce
tartar sauce
Directions
Cut the lemons and onions in half, cut the sausage into1 inch pieces, then cut corn into thirds. Bring the water to a boil in a

large pot. Squeeze the lemon juice into the water and then throw the lemon halves in the pot. Add onion, garlic, salt and Old Bay seasoning. Reduce heat to medium-low, cover and simmer for 10 minutes. Add the potatoes, corn and sausage, and return to a boil. Simmer covered for 30 minutes. Remove from heat, stir in the shrimp, and cover for 5 minutes. Drain off the liquid before serving. Serve with cocktail or tartar sauce and crackers.

Fruit Compote In Foil

Ingredients
sliced pineapple
fresh blueberries
fresh strawberries
powdered sugar
whipped cream or sour cream
Directions
Place a slice of pineapple on a square of aluminum foil. Pile up some blueberries and strawberries on the top. Sprinkle with a little of the powdered sugar. Seal the fruit tightly in the foil. Heat about 10 to 15 minutes on the grill. To serve, fold foil back and top with the cream.
For curried fruit: Follow above recipe, except omit the powdered sugar and add 2 tablespoons butter and 1 teaspoon curry powder. Serve this with lamb or chicken.
For fruit with mint: Follow the above recipe. Heat chopped mint (10 leaves or so) in a 1 tablespoon of water. Bruise the mint (crush it with the back of a spoon against the side of the pan). Strain the leaves off and pour the flavored water over the fruit. Continue to warm through.

Fruit Kabobs

Ingredients
any assorted fruits
1 choney
2 tsplemon juice
Directions
Thread on long skewers any combination of fresh, canned or dried fruits, using chunks about the same size. If using wooden skewers, soak for 1/2 hour in water before threading on fruit. Try pineapple chunks, dried apricots (soak in water first to plump), peach haves, etc. Brush with honey thinned with a little lemon juice. Grill over low heat until hot. Brush them with butter as they are grilling, if desired. Serve with the leftover hot honey sauce.

Garbage

Ingredients
1 dozen eggs
12 - 16oz. Jimmie Dean Sausage (Hot)
1 diced tomato
1 chopped green bell pepper
1 chopped red bell pepper
1/4cchopped onion
1 clove garlic, pressed
tortillas
Directions
In a Large pot, cook sausage until done. Add bell peppers, onion and garlic, cook until tender. Add diced tomatoes and cook for another 5-7 min. Fry eggs (over easy). Serve sausage mixture into individual servings and place 1-2 fried eggs over serving. Serve with warm flour or corn tortillas.

Tip: Cut veggies ahead of time and place in zip lock baggies and place in cooler before leaving for trip.

Girl Scouts Banana Dessert

Ingredients
Banana
Chocolate chips
Carob chips
mini marshmallows
nuts, chopped
Directions
My favorite dessert was foil-wrapped. We would slice a banana lengthwise, and stuff it w/chocolate or carob chips, mini marshmallows, and chopped nuts for some. Wrap it up good in the foil, and place on the hot coals in the campfire pit, generally for about 10-15 minutes. It is the best!

Golden Parmesan Potatoes

Ingredients
6large potatoes
1/4cflour
1/4cParmesan cheese, grated
3/4tspsalt
1/2tsppepper
1/3cbutter
Directions
Peel potatoes and cut into cubes. Use a Ziploc bag and combine flour, cheese, salt and pepper. Place wet potatoes in bag and shake until well coated. Melt butter in 9 x 13 inch pan. Place potatoes in pan and bake at 425 degrees for 1 hour. Turn potatoes several times. This can be done in an oven or over a camp stove.

Gorp

Ingredients
1 1/2cPlanters Dry Roasted Peanuts
1 1/2cDel Monte Diced Dried Fruit Mix
6 oz. package semisweet chocolate chips
Directions
Combine peanuts, dried fruit and chocolate chips. Toss well. Store in airtight container.

Grandma's Easy Camping Taco

Ingredients
ground beef
taco seasoning
1 jar quesadilla cheese or shredded cheese
sour cream
salsa
lettuce
tomatoes
individual bags of corn chips
Directions
Fry the ground beef and add the taco seasoning and ½ of the salsa. Crunch the bags of corn chips open along the side, place a spoon of taco mix on top of the chips in bag and add cheese, more salsa and sour cream and enjoy!
You can spice the meat however you want and add whatever ingredients to make the taco interesting, green chilies ar

Great Omelet

Ingredients

1-2eggs
milk
bacon
onions
green, red, and yellow or orange peppers
celery
cheese
dill pickles (if desired)
salt & pepper (and garlic powder if desired)
Directions
You will need a cast iron pot or frying pan. Dice and saute bacon lightly, add all veggies and saute lightly. Mix eggs, milk, salt, pepper and garlic powder, dill pickles, add to sauted bacon and veggies. Cover and cook slowly (preferably over campfire). Cook time depends on how much you make. When almost cooked, cover with cheese and let melt for 15-30 minutes. Serve with toast.

Grilled Apple Rings

Ingredients
apples
granulated sugar
brown sugar
cinnamon
butter or margarine
Directions
Core crisp apples. Do not peel. Cut in crosswise 1 inch slices. Brush with margarine or butter and lay carefully on the grill. Grill about 8 minutes on one side about 4 to 6 inches from the coals. Turn and sprinkle on the sugar and cinnamon. The sugar will melt while the other side is browning. Continue grilling until the apple rings are tender and browned.

Grilled Apples In Apple Brandy

Ingredients
6 - 8 fresh apples
Apple Brandy
Powdered Sugar
Directions
Just before serving, slice the fresh apples. Place in the center of a square of heavy aluminum foil. Drizzle with a little apple brandy and seal the packages tightly to prevent leagage. Place foil packages over hot coals and cook 4 - 5 minutes.
To serve, open foil and sprinkle apples with powdered sugar.

Grilled Bbq Meatloaf

Ingredients
3 pound(s) ground beef
1 box Pork Stove Top Stuffing
3 eggs
3/4c BBQ sauce
1/2c water
2 tsp garlic powder
1 tsp salt (optional)
1 tsp pepper
Directions
Mix together above ingredients. Form into a loaf. Place in an aluminum Hot Bag. Pour a layer of BBQ sauce over the top of the loaf. Salt and pepper and more garlic powder also if desired. Seal Bag. Place on a rack over hot coals. Flip bag every now and then. Grill until done (aprox. 1 hour). Enjoy!

Grilled Breakfast Sandwich

Ingredients
4eggs
1/4cmilk
2 - 4slices of ham
2 - 4slices of cheese
4 - 6slices of bread
Directions
Mix eggs, pour in milk and mix together. Dip bread in mixture, both sides. cook on grill till golden. Use enough bread slices till all egg mixture is gone. Take slice of cheese (I use cheddar and cut in thick slice) take slice of thick black forest ham. Add cheese and ham in-between 2 slices of cooked bread mixture. Cut in half and serve with syrup.

Grilled Marinated Shark Steaks

Ingredients
1 pound(s) fresh shark steaks (or tuna, salmon, flounder, etc.)
4ounce Kraft Zesty Italian Dressing
shredded colby and monterrey jack cheese
Directions
Place the shark steaks and the dressing inside a ziplock bag. Marinating time is entirely up to you, 2 hours to 2 days!! Grill the steaks until opaque. Garnish with shredded colby and monterrey jack cheese. Enjoy with fresh grilled vegetables on the side.

Grilled Peanut Butter Sandwiches

Ingredients
Peanut butter
Sliced bread
Butter

Chocolate chips (optional)
Directions
Spread peanut butter on one piece of bread and put another slice on top to make a sandwich. Butter the outsides and cook on skillet till golden brown. Flip and do same to other side. Chocolate chips can be added to the peanut butter if desired.

Grilled Peppers

Ingredients
12 Jalapeno peppers
1 package bacon
1 12 oz. package cream cheese
1 8 oz. package Pepper Jack cheese
Directions
Cut peppers in half long way (clean out seeds and veins). Fill with cream cheese and a piece of pepper jack cheese. Wrap with bacon and secure with toothpicks. Place on grill or fire grate until bacon looks done and cool and Enjoy! These are great as appetizers or any time.

Grilled Pineapple

Ingredients
1 fresh whole pineapple
1 stick butter
1 tsp cinnamon
Directions
Cut pineapple in half, then into wedges, discarding the outer part. Melt butter and add cinnamon. Grill on medium heat, basting with butter and cinnamon. Ready when fruit turns golden brown and has softened.

Grilled Pizza

Ingredients
burrito size tortillas
1 can tomato/pizza sauce
shredded mozzarella cheese (or your favorite)
grilled chicken or vegetable toppings (optional)
Directions
Prepare pizza by pouring an even layer of sauce on the burrito to create the pizza shell or crust. Place cheese and toppings on the burrito. Spray campfire rack or camping grill with cooking spray to prevent tortilla from sticking. Cover for approximately 5-7 minutes or until cheese melts and burrito lightly browns.

Grilled Potatoes

Ingredients
2pound(s)red potatoes, quartered or cut into pieces
1/4cbutter, melted
2cloves minced garlic
1 tspseasoning salt
Directions
Combine butter, garlic and seasoned salt in bowl and pour over cut potatoes. Place seasoned potatoes into an 8-inch or larger disposable aluminum pan and cover with foil (or create your own aluminum packet from heavy duty foil wrap).
Grill potatoes over medium heat 35 to 45 minutes, stirring the potatoes in the pan or flipping the foil packet.

Grilled Shrimp

Ingredients

1 pound(s)medium raw shrimp, peeled all but the tails
1 Tbspolive oil
Old Bay seasoning
Directions
Place shrimp in a zip lock bag and add Olive Oil and sprinkle with Old Bay Seasoning. Let marinate at least half hour or longer. Grill shrimp either on skewers or a grill pan a few minutes on each side until pink, grill should be on low setting. Serve with French bread and grilled vegetables.

Grilled Squash & Zucchini

Ingredients
4squash (sliced lengthwise)
4zucchini (sliced lenghtwise)
green bell pepper (diced)
1 small white onioin (diced)
4Tbspbutter
2 TbspMrs. Dash seasoning
2 Tbspgarlic, minced
Directions
Place one half each squash and zucchini on square of foil. Cover with bell peppers and onions, 1/2 pat of butter and Mrs. Dash seasoning. Fold foil top down, and seal the ends. Place foil pouches on Swing Grill and cook for about 30 to 35 minutes over medium low heat.

Grilled Squash

Ingredients
2-3yellow summer squash
2-3zucchini
1 onion
Italian dressing

Directions
Slice the yellow summer squash and zucchini, then cut up the onion. Marinate in Italtian dressing. Cover grill with foil, (or use grilling rack). Put Veggeis on grill, turn occasionally and cook until tender, then salt and pepper to taste.

Grilled Vegies

Ingredients
green and yellow zucchini
red and green peppers
onions, chopped
citrus marinade
Directions
Slice green and yellow zucchini, red and green peppers and chopped onions, marinate in citrus marinade, and wrap in tin foil. Then place on the grill and let steam until almost cooked. Open foil and brush marinade on vegies and grill until soft.

Gringo Gordy's Grilled Veggies

Ingredients
fresh produce
olive oil
seasoning salt
parmesan cheese
Directions
Get all the fresh produce you can find from the side road market, leave the skin on and cut in quarters or eights. Splash with olive oil and add Mrs. Dash or Lowry's Seasoning Salt and parmesean cheese. Grill on open fire or grill until grill marks appear.

Ham & Sweet Potato Foil Packets

Ingredients
cubed ham
cubed sweet potatoes
1/2 apple, cubed
Directions
Place all ingredients in a foil, seal tightly Cook on hot coals for approx. 1/2 hour turning every 15 min.

Hamburger Hobo Pie

Ingredients
1 1/2 pound(s) ground chuck or ground beef
1 medium onion, thickly sliced
6 - 8 medium sized carrots, cut into chunks
6 red potatoes, cut into wedges
seasoning salt
Directions
Spray a large piece of heavy duty foil (or the Reynolds foil bags) with no stick spray. On the foil, scatter vegetables, and break up ground meat and loosely mix together (do not pack or smash together). Sprinkle liberally with seasoning salt (or other spices you prefer to use). Fold the foil into a pouch, making sure all ends are tightly crimped together. Place foil packet onto grill grate if you are grilling, or onto a grate over a campfire. Do not put foil packet directly onto coals as the foil will burn through. Now for the tricky part: turning it over and knowing when the food is done. I use heavy duty grilling tongs and an old oven mitt to turn - watch for the grease leaking out of the foil packet so that it doesn't cause a flame flare-up. When the potatoes are soft, then everything else is cooked. I usually push on the packet and if I feel a potato smash, then I know everything is done. Or

you can open the side of the packet and test a potato with a knife. Cooking time is approximately 30 minutes, depending on the how hot your fire or grill is. My family prefers the vegetables to be on the burnt side, and we all fight over the veggies that burn onto the foil! Just take the packet off the fire, put onto heat proof surface, and cut an X into the top of the packet and open up. Watch the steam! And enjoy!!!!

Alternative veggies: fresh green beans, bell pepper slices, fresh corn cut off the cob, a clove or two of garlic, thick chunks of squash.

Hamburger Stew

Ingredients
1 1/2pound(s)ground beef or turkey
1-2ccarrots
1 medium onion
4-5medium potatoes
1 bag frozen peas
1 package onion soup mix
water
salt and pepper
oregano or basil
Directions
Brown the meat in a large pot or dutch oven. Chop up the carrots, onion and potatoes and add them, then add the onion soup mix with enough water to cover. Cover the pot and simmer until the potatoes are tender (about 20-30 minutes). Add the peas to the pot. Season to taste with salt, pepper and oregano or basil. Simmer until the peas are hot. Serve with a loaf of warm French or sourdough bread. To make cooking time easier at camp, you can cook the meat and freeze it at home.

Hamburger-Rice Casserole

Ingredients
1 pound(s) hamburger
2 onions
1 c diced celery
2 Tbsp butter
2 Tbsp soya sauce
1 can cream of mushroom soup
1/2 c cooked rice
1 can chicken rice soup
1 c water

Directions
Bake at 250 degrees for 1 1/2 hours. Sprinkle Chinese noodles on top.

Hash Brown Casserole

Ingredients
2 pound(s) frozen hash browns
1 16 ounce sour cream
1 can cream of chicken soup
1 stick butter
1/2 c green onions (chopped)
2 c sharp cheddar cheese (grated)
1 can French fried onions

Directions
Place potatoes in a large bowl and season with salt and pepper. Melt butter, combine with green onions, sour cream, soup and 1 cup of cheddar cheese. Mix together well and add hash browns. Pour into oiled Dutch oven; ring top with French fried onions and fill the center with cheese. Hang on medium hook over low fire and bake for 45 minutes, or until potatoes are completely

warm and cheese melts. Oven directions: 350° for 45 minutes in 9 x 13 inch pan.

Heather's Campfire Chicken Parmesan

Ingredients
6chicken nuggets (thawed)
1/8cshredded low-fat mozzarella cheese
1/4cspaghetti sauce
parmesan cheese
oregano or Italian seasoning

Directions
On a square piece of foil, place the thawed chicken nuggets. Pour the spaghetti sauce on top of the nuggets. Spread cheese on top of nuggets and sprinkle with parmesan and season to taste. Cook over campfire until cheese is melted and nuggets heated through (about 10-15 minutes). Open and enjoy!

Hildebrandt Family Campfire Potatoes

Ingredients
2Cans whole new potatoes
2Cloves minced garlic
4tspOlive Oil
4tspButter
Salt
Pepper
Directions
You will need four 8 inch long pieces of foil. Place in the middle of each foil piece a half a can of potatoes, 1/4 of the garlic, some salt, a little pepper, and 1 teaspoon of each butter and olive oil. Wrap the foil up with the mixture and throw directly into the fire. Cook for 15. Let stand a few mins and the enjoy!

Hillbilly Stew

Ingredients
1 pound(s)ground venison or beef
1 large onion (chopped)
1 large can Campbell's Pork and Beans
1 small can Campbell's Pork and Beans
1 Tbspmolasses
2 Tbspbutter
Directions
In a cast iron skillet, melt butter, add onions, cook until they start to turn clear. Brown meat, open cans of beans and drain the small can only. Add to browned mixture and simmer for about 20 minutes until beans are hot. Serve over mashed potatoes.

Hobo Burgers

Ingredients
hamburger
onion, sliced
yellow squash, sliced
potatoes, sliced
mushrooms
carrots, sliced
zuchini, sliced
Directions
Make Hamburger patties as normal. Place each on a piece of foil. Add to foil any or all of the following: sliced onion, sliced yellow squash, sliced potatoes, fresh mushrooms, sliced carrots, or sliced zuchini. Add salt and pepper to season. Add a pat of

margarine. Roll foil to close. Cook over campfire or grill until veggies and burger are done. Open foil and enjoy!

Hobo Chicken

Ingredients
1 boneless, skinless chicken breast
sweet corn
button mushrooms
green beans
baby carrots
small red potatoes
sweet onions
1 cwater
seasoning salt

Directions
You will need a strip of heavy duty aluminum foil wrap to make a bag (or get Hot Bags) for each person. Everyone can make their own meal by putting a chicken breast and the vegetables that they like in the bag, add the water and some seasoning salt, close the bag, put a name on them and put it on a hot fire pit for about an hour. Enjoy!!!

Hobo Dinner

Makes: 20
Ingredients
5pound(s)Kielbasa or Italian Sausag
5pound(s)small potatoes (clean but not peeled
3pound(s)carrots (scrubbed)
3pound(s)onions (peeled but left whole)
3Heads of Cabbage (quartered

12ears of Sweet Corn (broke in half
Salt
Pepper
Garlic
Directions
You only need to add about 1/4 kettle full of water before placing on the heat and cover. We usually layer with the carrots and Kielbasa on the bottom to start cooking first. Cabbage on top so it doesn't fall apart in the process of cooking. You want it to simmer for about 2 hours. Be sure to have a long handled spoon/ladle to dish out. Season to taste. Yummy!

Hobo Potatoes

Ingredients
5medium potatoes (wash, but do not peel)
1 large onion (chopped)
4slice(s)bacon
salt and pepper
garlic. if desired (chopped)
2 Tbspbutter or margarine or 1 Tbsp olive oil
Directions
You will need a large sheet of heavy duty aluminum foil, or double the normal foil. Put the bacon slices side-by-side in the center of the aluminum foil. Cut the potatoes into cubes (1/2 to 3/4 inch square) and put on top of the bacon. Top potatoes with onion and seasonings. Dab with cut up butter, or drizzle olive oil over the top. Fold aluminum foil and seal all edges. Place on pre-heated gas or charcoal grill for 30-40 minutes. Cut foil open across the top (watch out for hot steam). Serves 2-4. A great companion to steak, burgers, pork chops, chicken, you name it!

Hobo Squares

Makes: 4
Ingredients
4 medium potatoes
8 carrots
1 1/2 pound(s) hamburger
large onion
8 slice(s) bacon
cooking oil spray
salt and pepper
Directions
Cut the potatoes into long slices and the carrots into slices. Divide the hamburger into 4 patties. Cut the onion into rings. Take a large sheet of tin foil, fold in half. Spray the inside with cooking spray. Place 2 slices of bacon on the bottom half and the hamburger patty on top of the bacon. Place a handful of carrots and a handful of potatoes and add several slices of onion to the packet. Salt and pepper entire packet. Seal the packet by folding the tinfoil around the edges. With a marker place a "U" on the top. This will help you remember which side is up. Place packets on a grille with either charcoal for heat or wood. Cook over medium heat for 15 minutes then turn over and cook for 10 more minutes. Open packets carefully and enjoy. Hobos are inexpensive to cook and kids as well as adults enjoy the taste.

www.ingramcontent.com/pod-product-compliance
Lightning Source LLC
Chambersburg PA
CBHW071433070526
44578CB00001B/95